Mentoring Students of Color

# Breakthroughs in the Sociology of Education

*Series Editor*

George W. Noblit (*Joseph R. Neikirk Distinguished Professor of Sociology of Education Emeritus*)

VOLUME 11

The titles published in this series are listed at *brill.com/bsed*

# Mentoring Students of Color

*Naming the Politics of Race, Social Class, Gender, and Power*

*Edited by*

Juan F. Carrillo, Danielle Parker Moore and Tim Conder

BRILL
SENSE

LEIDEN | BOSTON

All chapters in this book have undergone peer review.

The Library of Congress Cataloging-in-Publication Data is available online at http://catalog.loc.gov

Typeface for the Latin, Greek, and Cyrillic scripts: "Brill". See and download: brill.com/brill-typeface.

ISSN 2665-9646
ISBN 978-90-04-40795-4 (paperback)
ISBN 978-90-04-40796-1 (hardback)
ISBN 978-90-04-40798-5 (e-book)

Copyright 2019 by Koninklijke Brill NV, Leiden, The Netherlands.
Koninklijke Brill NV incorporates the imprints Brill, Brill Hes & De Graaf, Brill Nijhoff, Brill Rodopi,
Brill Sense, Hotei Publishing, mentis Verlag, Verlag Ferdinand Schöningh and Wilhelm Fink Verlag.
All rights reserved. No part of this publication may be reproduced, translated, stored in a retrieval system,
or transmitted in any form or by any means, electronic, mechanical, photocopying, recording or otherwise,
without prior written permission from the publisher.
Authorization to photocopy items for internal or personal use is granted by Koninklijke Brill NV provided
that the appropriate fees are paid directly to The Copyright Clearance Center, 222 Rosewood Drive, Suite
910, Danvers, MA 01923, USA. Fees are subject to change.

This book is printed on acid-free paper and produced in a sustainable manner.

# Contents

Notes on Contributors   VII

Introduction   1
  *Juan F. Carrillo and Tim Conder*

1  Capitalizing on Achievement: A Critical Examination of School-Based
   Mentoring Programs and Student Achievement   13
     *Shanyce L. Campbell*

2  Someone Fabulous Like Me: White Mentors' Representations of Moralities
   and Possibilities for a White Complicity Pedagogy for Mentoring   36
     *Amy Senta and Danielle Parker Moore*

3  Class Crossings: Mentoring, Stratification and Mobility   62
     *George Noblit, Danielle Parker Moore and Amy Senta*

4  "I Don't Think It's Changed Me, It's Helped Mold Me": The Agency of
   Students of Color in a Whitestream Mentoring Organization   89
     *Tim Conder and Alison LaGarry*

5  Inculcando *Confianza*: Towards Exploring the Possibilities in the
   Mentoring of Latina Youth   118
     *Esmeralda Rodriguez*

6  Examining the Mentoring Discourse Regarding the Parenting Practices of
   Black, Female-Led Families   145
     *Dana Griffin*

7  Final Thoughts   163
     *Juan F. Carrillo*

# Notes on Contributors

*Shanyce L. Campbell*
received her Ph.D. in Public Policy at the University of North Carolina at Chapel Hill and a Bachelor's of Science (summa cum laude) in Accounting with a concentration in Economics from North Carolina A&T State University. Dr. Campbell is an assistant professor at the University of California, Irvine School of Education. Her research focuses on understanding how policies and practices influence access to quality learning opportunities for students marginalized by the educational system.

*Juan F. Carrillo*
is an associate professor at the Mary Lou Fulton Teachers College. Dr. Carrillo received a Ph.D. Curriculum and Instruction, Cultural Studies in Education, University of Texas–Austin. Carrillo's interdisciplinary research draws from critical frameworks and qualitative methodologies such as narrative inquiry, autoethnography, and testimonios. His work looks at the role of agency in historically marginalized communities, with a particular focus on Latinx students. One of his focus areas is on the schooling trajectories of academically successful Latino males that come from working-class origins.

*Tim Conder*
recently received his Ph.D. from the University of North Carolina Chapel Hill in Culture, Curriculum, and Change with an interdisciplinary cultural studies focus. His primary focus of research has been on the intersection of race and other regimes of oppression, religion (as a repressive or liberative space), and practiced identities of social justice activism. He currently teaches as an Assistant Adjunct Professor at the University of North Carolina at Chapel Hill.

*Dana Griffin*
received a Ph.D. in Counselor Education from College of William and Mary. Dr. Griffin is Associate Professor at The University of North Carolina at Chapel Hill. Dr. Griffin's research interest is in parent involvement and family-school-community collaboration and feels that such collaboration can be better achieved when people are multiculturally competent and understand the different minutia of families and parenting

*Alison LaGarry*
received a Ph.D. in Education from the University of North Carolina at Chapel Hill in 2016, and specialized in the Culture, Curriculum, and Change strand

of study. She holds a Master of Music degree in Music Education from Ithaca College, as well as a baccalaureate degree from the same institution in Vocal Performance and Music Education. LaGarry has varied public and private school teaching experience in a number of U.S. cities including Boston, MA and Washington, DC. She has partnered with a several prominent organizations including the Children's Defense Fund and the Metropolitan Opera Guild to implement educational initiatives. Alison is the co-editor of *Possibilities in Practice: Social Justice Teaching in the Disciplines* (Peter Lange, 2017).

### George Noblit

received a Ph.D. in Sociology at the University of Oregon. He is a Joseph R. Neikirk Distinguished Professor of Sociology of Education, University of North Carolina, Chapel Hill. school desegregation, with a program of research on the social construction of race, using ethnographic research to study schools and other educational scenes. Noblit, with co-author Dwight Hare in their 1988 publication of "Meta-Ethnography: Synthesizing Qualitative Studies," developed a research method for gathering and analyzing data from multiple qualitative studies to uncover patterns unseen in individual studies. Since then, the meta-ethnography process has been cited by more than 2,800 scholars and is now used in other fields, including in the study of health services.

### Danielle Parker Moore

received a Ph.D. from The University of North Carolina at Chapel Hill. Her research is focused on black mothers experiences of out of school enrichment programs. She an Assistant Professor of Education at Wake Forest University where she also serves as the Executive Director of the Wake Forest University Freedom School Summer Program.

### Esmeralda Rodriguez

is originally from the Rio Grande Valley in on the Texas/Mexico border. She earned a Ph.D. in Cultural Studies and Literacies from the University of North Carolina, Chapel Hill. Her research engages critical ethnographic approaches to the study of identities, intersectionalities, and education. She draws on critical pedagogy, border pedagogy, and Chicana feminist thought and pedagogies to analyze of how intersections of race, ethnicity, class, and gender reveal systemic inequities in education and generate critically reflexive and transformative literacies and pedagogies in Latina youth and their families. She is currently a Language Development Specialist in North Carolina.

NOTES ON CONTRIBUTORS

*Amy Senta*

received both her Ph.D. and her M.A. in Education in the area of culture, curriculum and change from the University of North Carolina. Senta's areas of research include participatory ethnography with youth in grades K-8, qualitative research methodologies, the social foundations of education, critical Whiteness studies, critical social theory, poststructuralism and cultural studies. Senta has published journal articles and book chapters that engage cultural studies with children's literature, critical Whiteness studies with programming for youth of color and social foundations of education with teacher education. She is currently working on a book project based on her dissertation, *Straining Silencing: Youth Film-Making on Schooling's Silencing*. That work brings together a post-critical ethnographic analysis with an agential realist poststructuralist reanalysis of four years of film-making with 24 youth on the topic of schooling's silencing.

# Introduction

*Juan F. Carrillo and Tim Conder*

Writing this introduction catalyzes many research-oriented questions and invokes many personal memories. Carrillo's scholarship has addressed the tenuous nature of "success" within Whitestream schooling settings among academically successful Latino males that come from working-class settings (Carrillo, 2013, 2016). Within this work, he has unpacked the narratives of gain and loss for youth of color engaged in trying to be "somebody" within traditional or hegemonic notions of achievement. Today, the idea of mentoring still triggers many mixed reactions and lingering critical questions. Mentoring rarely if ever examines how dominant group communities can "improve." How can we name and address *their* "achievement gaps"? Carrillo is a Chicano scholar that was raised on welfare in the barrios of Compton, California and neighboring communities. He was the first person in his immediate family to graduate from third grade. Moreover, Carrillo was groomed in the languages of the street, the library, and the ambivalent as well as tragicomedic ideas of "making-it." He often wondered if he went from one ghetto to another. In the wake of his own schooling journey, he still sees in his heart's glasses his mother's eyes, his father's back pain, and the rural communities in Mexico where they grew up. He still hears their stories, memories, love, and their sharing of precious knowledge. Schooling often felt like a separation from all that reality. School in some ways became a place where he was mentored on 'how to be' so that he can get a degree and 'get stuff'—like a house, access to a 'good neighborhood,' and hegemonic values.

A critical and relevant memory: Mexico City. 2010. Carrillo was at the airport. Delays. After about six hours of waiting, he began to wonder around eventually coming across a museum inside the airport. Within, there were artifacts from the local anthropology museum. He wandered through this space, learning about Mexico's indigenous roots—the legacy, history, and the "positives" related to his "culture." Feeling so inspired, so full of gratitude and pride, Carrillo started crying. He is part of the long arm of "accomplishments" of so many architects, writers, and spiritual geniuses. Yet, as soon as he flew back to Texas, he felt the emptiness of knowing that he was going to be once again mentored out of that legacy—back into invisibility and deficiency. It's more than disappointing.

We offer this backdrop as a means by which to share our own messy relationship with ideas around mentorship and its various gaps and even, positives.

© KONINKLIJKE BRILL NV, LEIDEN, 2019 | DOI: 10.1163/9789004407985_001

Nationwide, approximately 5 million youth are involved in some form of mentoring (McKenna, 1998). In this book, we do not take on an exhaustive focus on mentoring. Yet, this work offers an important glimpse into how mentoring can both be a productive space for youth to develop but also challenges the often-unquestioned assumptions related to how race, class, and gender and power may operate problematically within the mentoring process. This book then, is dedicated to all the youth of color who interact with a world in which their talents are mostly deemed invisible or insufficient. Mentoring may be one way to work around that tension, but, as this book attests, there are dire tradeoffs and contradictions in the process.

## 1 Literature Review

The act of mentoring predates any "publication" on the topic. The printed, English use of the term "mentoring," seems to derive from Ann Murry's 1778 publication, *Mentoria: The Young Ladies Instructor* (published by J. Fry & Co.). Moreover, the history of documented youth mentoring in the United States dates back to social movements in the 19th and early 20th centuries (Baker & Maguire, 2005; Freedman, 1993). Specifically, some of the first documented mentors came from the work of Jane Addams and her colleagues that helped usher in juvenile courts and inaugurate probation officers in the role of mentors (Baker & Maguire, 2005). Freedman (1993) suggests that youth mentoring has its origins in the Friendly Visiting Movement that utilized middle class volunteers to help serve as "role models" and provide support to poor families. Mentoring has largely worked under the premise of "helping" the "disadvantaged." For many mentors, this idea has moral underpinnings where volunteering and supporting people to achieve certain goals or acquire certain resources, opportunities, and/or protection is deemed as "the right thing" for them to do.

Yet through all the goodwill, there are persistent concerns related to mentoring. For one, historically, the literature reveals that there has been an emphasis on a top-down, vertical approach by mentors. This patriarchal posture has been critiqued by McGuire and Reger (2003). This style of mentoring assumes a "mentor knows best" and/or "be like me ... let me 'fix you'" approach without critically analyzing issues of power. It does not consider the potential of dialogical mentorship, where both mentor and mentee have something of value to share. Despite the strong emphasis on patriarchal and hierarchical norms in mentoring, McDougall and Beattie (1997) do discuss the potential benefits of *peer mentoring*. This is a reciprocal approach focusing on mentoring within the

INTRODUCTION

context of a dialogue among peers. Similarly, Goldner and Mayseless (2009) contend that it is important to build high-quality relationships in order to establish effective mentoring relationships. Tierney and Grossman (2000) also assert that mentoring programs can nurture caring relationships.

Second, there has been limited research on mentoring that takes into account race, ethnicity, class, and gender, and sexuality. An emerging wave of literature is beginning to address these concerns (see Dubois & Karcher, 2014). Sanchez, Colón-Torres, Feuer, Roundfield, and Berardi (2014) cite previous research that notes tension in cross-racial mentoring relationships (Schippers, 2008) and offer this warning about mentoring programs that regularly assign student mentees of color to White mentors:

> However, these very youth, who arguably are particularly in need of mentors and may be matched with one through programs, may for reasons that are fully understandable harbor feelings of mistrust toward adults who are not of the racial/ethnic group. Research along these lines is in its infancy, but it appears that cultural mistrust may sometimes inhibit the quality of the relationships that youth of color develop with adults to whom they are matched in programs. (p. 156)

This emerging research offers some urgency toward developing critical reflexivity in mentoring programs that may be color-blind and silence intentional discourse on race, while not fully appreciating the racial nature of mentoring in these cross-racial dyads.

Considering gender in youth mentoring, Liang, Bogat, and Duffy (2013) broach a key intersectional point in noting that the literature to this point has "focused disproportionately on the experience of middle-class, White, female and male mentors" (p. 169) and that gender research in mentoring may be far too prone to assuming homogeneity in gender and that "the real world tells us that boys and girls are unlikely to be homogenous groups" (p. 170). Their research moves the conversation toward more person-centered approaches especially in mentor relationship matching and highlights the strong need for far greater research on the impact of gender in mentoring relationships and the outcomes of mentoring relationships (Liang, Bogat, & Duffy, 2013).

Deutsch, Lawrence, and Henneberger (2014) make a similar case regarding social class saying, "We suspect that many programs would benefit from considering both the material and the cultural aspects of social class more explicitly in how they approach staff, mentor, and mentee recruitment and training" (p. 185). Noting that "social class offers a cultural context for understanding youth development; it shapes the environment in which youth and their families live as well as their values, beliefs, and practices" (Deutsch et al., 2014, p. 185), caution in mentor assignment and training is needed given that many mentoring relationships involve social class differences. They suggest that "the more cultural differences between mentors and mentees, the more mentors should first establish a sense of equal status and appreciation of cultural differences with their mentees before embarking on a change agenda" (Deutsch et al., 2014, p. 185). This second wave of mentoring research on race, gender, and social class beckons for an urgent escalation of intersectional socio-cultural critique in mentoring research.

Finally, youth mentoring is generally imagined as an approach to address "at risk" youth. This model is in many ways grounded in a deficit lens for it fails to note what communities of color bring to the mentoring process. Yet, other more asset-based approaches to interrogate the common structure of mentoring and its primary ideological assumptions are available. For instance, Liou, Martinez, and Rotheram-Fuller (2016) describe a critical mentoring vision with critical pedagogy as its core assumption which resists hierarchical paternalism in the mentoring relationship and hence taps into the students' *community cultural wealth* (Yosso, 2005). This mentoring approach also draws from Freirian (1993) philosophy. For instance, they describe Freire's work in the context on their mentoring orientation:

> We argue that the intrinsic benefits of a top-down relationship are not in the interest of the mentee, but the mentor, and such a relationship has the possibility to harbor deficit ideologies and cause more harm when the mentee resists the confines of that vision. Therefore, the liberatory approach encourages self-determination in the mentee to fully utilize his or her agency to inform, empower, and transform lived realities. (p. 108)

Mentoring, as such, has the potential to form a dialogue that awakens all participants into the liberatory aspects of humanization and provides a much a stronger critique of power. Moreover, as Valenzuela (1999) suggests, authentic caring requires that we center the assets and cultural knowledge that comes from the students' communities versus approaching them through a deficit lens.

## 2     The Gold Medal (GM) Mentoring Program

For the purpose of this book, we use the pseudonym, *Gold Medal* for the mentoring program that we discuss herein. These chapters are also part of larger process where a team of faculty and graduate students from the University of

INTRODUCTION

North Carolina -Chapel Hill took part in an evaluation of the GM Program. Our evaluation report consisted of quantitative and qualitative results. Some of the more detailed findings are evident in the chapters that follow. However, here are 5 key findings from the evaluation:

1. GM is a well-designed mentoring program. It meets and exceeds the 'best practices' established by research on youth mentoring programs.
2. GM is extremely effective in promoting high school graduation and college attendance.
3. GM has significant effects on grade point average of the students, but not on test scores. This finding represents a challenge to the school district. How can the motivation and classroom work of these students be converted into improved test scores?
4. Parents, mentors, and mentees all highly value the program and see it as effective. Nevertheless, race and language are issues that participants find themselves continuing to struggle with in the school district.
5. Program staff also highly value the program and, through a commitment toward continuous improvement, work to make the program more effective for program participants. However, the level of staffing seems minimal for the tasks required and consequently relies heavily on part-time, temporary and volunteer personnel.

Based on these findings, the evaluation team concluded that GM Mentoring is "an important asset" to the school district. It was highly effective for youth and their families; it provided the district with a conduit to families that have been traditionally hard for the schools to serve well.

These findings led to a series of considerations for the program staff and for the school district. The report, when presented to the school board, was received very well and the program was invited to submit a proposal for increased funding. In all, then, we argue the program was successful. This success, in turn, directs the critiques we offer in this book more specifically to the broader *phenomenon* of school-based youth mentoring. These critical analysis speaks to how the *phenomenon* of school-based youth mentoring is embedded in wider social patterns that promote inequity and entail misrepresentation of the youth, mentors and their families.

Additionally, here are some basic stats about the Gold Medal Program:
– 97.5% of Gold Medal students have graduated from high school
– Many of GM's high school graduates have enrolled in post-secondary education
– 90% of the mentoring relationships last for 2 years or more
– 60% of graduates have had the same mentor from fourth grade through high school graduation

– Over 95% of our students, parents, and mentors rated GM as "excellent" or "good" in a 2010 program evaluation

Gold Medal is based in a North Carolina region that has a large college-educated population with a high cost of living. In fact, over 77% of the population has a bachelor's degree and 44% hold a graduate degree. Many reputable universities are located in this region, including Duke University, the University of North Carolina at Chapel Hill, and North Carolina State University. Moreover, the area is deemed by locals as being a "liberal" or "progressive" community. Yet, there are many issues as it pertains to addressing equity issues in its local schools and broader concerns around social justice in the larger community. There is a growing Latinx population and a small African American student body in the area's schools, both typically accounting for less than 15 percent of the student body. The local school district is generally considered to be a top-performing district, but does have considerable issues related to the achievement of students of color and English language learners. The Gold Medal Mentoring Program pairs students of color from 4th grade through high school with mentors from this primarily White privileged community. Indeed, most of the assigned mentors are White and come from middle to upper middle class backgrounds. In addition to the support and advocacy from their mentors, mentees receive access to special programing and curriculum.

## 3    Critical Perspectives

Mentoring is often embedded in unequal power relations. There is nothing neutral about the intent and practice of mentoring youth. While acknowledging good intentions at the core of many programs, mentoring is situated in power imbalances, the centering of certain values over others and uneasy tensions around race and ethnicity, class, gender, and sexuality. Programs also sometimes fail to engage assumptions about how we decide what counts as education and who gets to mentor whom. As such, there is often a structure where the dominant group teaches students of color their values and strategies so that they can be "successful" like them. Mentees are often framed as deficient and in needing of "fixing" by professional "White saviors." There is a long global and U.S. history of these kinds of power interactions by hegemonic interests. Property, power, values, identity, morality, and "progress" are often marked by specific decisions around what matters and needs to be replicated. Funding, assessments, curriculum, alienation, and marginalization can all be shaped consciously and unconsciously by these mandates.

INTRODUCTION

Acknowledging these tensions, this book explores both challenges and opportunities within the mentoring process. It is our contention that we need to tap into the community cultural wealth (Yosso, 2005) of students of color and acknowledge how working-class students of color often navigate multiple cultural worlds in "gifted" ways (Carrillo, 2016). Additionally, we need to center the importance of reciprocity and critical dialogue in mentoring (i.e. Freire, 1993). As such, we need to imagine a more liberatory praxis of mentoring and encourage the development of critical hope (Duncan-Andrade, 2009) versus non-critical college access rhetoric that may not be aligned with community goals, legacies, or multiple ways of living and imagining the human experience. Simply put, students of color possess valuable knowledge and have a lot to teach White mentors. Mentoring should not be a colonial exercise in subtractive "dream building." These issues must be at the forefront of mentor training, dialogue about the structure of mentoring, and the development of a mentoring curriculum that attempts to be critical of an ethnocentric gaze of the "other."

Our critiques *contextualize* the GM program and thus speak more broadly and with more significance than the mere generalizability that mentoring allows. Our critiques have a level of significance that many program critiques cannot claim, because they are based on evaluation findings from a successful program. This critique of a successful and highly appreciated program by mentors, mentees, mentee families, and the school district speaks directly to the broader *phenomenon* of school-based youth mentoring programs and the problematic aspects of this phenomenon. Our critiques reveal how the inequities and misrepresentations writ large of our wider society are intrinsically embedded in youth mentoring. And, these critiques establish significant concerns even when school-based youth mentoring programs are "done well," meaning when they produce highly amenable results for all concerned parties including educators, administrators, mentors, mentored students of color, and their families.

We still submit that youth mentoring does do good things. But, in doing good things, it also reproduces the issues that call for mentoring programs in the first place. Thus the question becomes not 'how to do good,' but also how to be less reproductive of existing social inequities and misrepresentations. Individual programs will vary in their particular instantiation of these reproductions and thus the *degree* of applicability of these critiques, but our approach here indicates that the phenomenon of school-based youth mentoring programs has embedded within itself the very inequities and misrepresentations or social concerns it seeks to ameliorate.

## 4    Chapter Summaries

This book is made up of six chapters. Below are brief summaries of each contribution.

Chapter 1, *Capitalizing on Achievement: A Critical Examination of School-Based Mentoring Programs and Student Achievement,* by Shanyce L. Campbell, uses a mixed methods approach to explore the effectiveness of the Gold Medal mentoring program. Shanyce's chapter offers important findings related to the links between tests scores and GM, examining the role of networks and cultural capital while also interrogating the role of race in the mentoring process.

Chapter 2, *Someone Fabulous Like Me: White Mentors' Representations of Moralities and Possibilities for a White Complicity Pedagogy for Mentoring* by Amy Senta and Danielle Park Moore uses Applebaum's (2010) theory of morality to examine how the mentorship of students of color draws from White notions of objectivity, emotions, and moral responsibility. The authors offer a critique of White complicity and offer some suggestions on how to move toward an antiracist approach to mentorship.

Chapter 3, *Class Crossings: Mentoring, Stratification and Mobility* by George Noblit, Danielle Park Moore and Amy Senta critically interrogates the role of social class in Gold Medal's mentoring program. The authors contend that we need to unpack the role of symbolic violence in mentoring, provide more in-depth considerations into traps of class-based value transmission, and emphasize the social capital aspects of mentoring relationships.

Chapter 4, *"I Don't Think It's Changed Me, It's Helped Mold Me": The Agency of Students of Color in a Whitestream Mentoring Organization* by Tim Conder and Alison LaGarry, uses a practice theory of identity (Holland, Lachicotte, Skinner, & Cain, 1998) to examine the multiple sites of identity production within the Gold Medal mentoring program. The authors use data from mentees to assert the ongoing agency of mentored students despite the racial colonization inherent in Whitestream mentoring structures.

Chapter 5, *Inculcando* Confianza: *Towards Exploring the Possibilities of Mentoring of Latina Youth* by Esmeralda Rodriguez, examines possibilities for creating community-centric solidarity versus paternalistic, classist, and top down approaches to mentoring. She offers a potential roadmap toward creating sacred spaces within the mentoring of Latina youth.

Chapter 6, *The Mentoring Discourse Regarding Parenting Practices of Black, Single Mothers* by Dana Griffin, examines the problematic discourses and approach toward Black mothers in the GM mentoring program. While acknowledging some of the benefits of GM, Griffin critically unpacks how

INTRODUCTION

African American mothers are silenced in the mentoring process and how White middle-class norms guide the mentoring relationship. She offers a powerful framework for developing trust with Black mothers and bringing their ways of knowing out of the shadows in mentoring programs.

Ultimately, all of these chapters offer critiques and, in some cases, suggestions for the improvement of the mentoring process. The authors acknowledge the power dimensions embedded in mentoring and they tease out the role we all have in being reflexive about how these programs function. What is clear is how the authors unpack the non-neutral values that make up any mentoring program.

## 5     A Call to Action

This book offers a call to action: we advocate for youth mentoring for social change versus an uncritical indoctrination into the status quo. There is so much that mentoring can do in terms of teaching youth about how to see, read, and name the ideological underpinnings of even (or especially) good will programs and processes which so often mask the status quo, colonizing assumptions of a Whitestream society. This "seeing, reading, and naming" implies the development of critical literacies among mentees and their families that can be aligned with a mentoring mission that focuses on encouraging mentees to read in their own interests (Carmangian, 2013).

As the chapters will demonstrate, parents and communities need to have a bigger role in creating mentoring programs in their own image. Moreover, this book illustrates the need for more awareness of and subsequent training related to the role of mentoring in perpetuating current structures and discourses as it relates to achievement and 'success.' We support a critical understanding of the role of power in defining the mentoring relationship. Within this greater awareness of power, issues of race, class, language, and 'values,' should be interrogated in light of persistent hegemonic conditions and assumptions. There is also the issue of 'culture,' the ways in which mentoring can serve as a dehumanizing process where the whole person is not welcomed but instead is 'fixed' out of its ways of knowing. It is important document and fully incorporate the funds of knowledge (Moll, Amanti, & Gonzalez, 1992) of families and communities in a mentoring vision. These stories need to be central to the issues and programming within a mentoring program.

This is part of what we hope that the reader will consider and these are some of the key issues that are brought forth in this book. The mentoring process is messy, hopeful, and, in some ways, violent. The chapters that follow will show that. Nonetheless, we cannot hide from the responsibility that we all have in making mentoring more reflexive and committed to a vision that is less paternalistic and subtractive and more open to a holistic, additive, and critical orientation.

## 6 Final Thoughts: Mentorship for What?

> Figure out how technologies operate. Use a wrench. Technologies can be disrupted and reorganized-at least for a machine cycle. Rather than just thinking of ourselves as just subjects of those technologies, think … how we might operate on ourselves and other technologies and turn these gears into decolonizing operations. (paperson, 2017, p. 24)

We end this introduction by wondering about the role of activist aesthetics: how can mentoring be connected to social justice? How can a mentoring program that does well in terms of academics add an emancipatory vision and practice into its programming? Is there a political project beyond academic success for students of color within mentoring programs? What other worlds are possible?

While we understand the pragmatic dimension of academic support, North Carolina, like many other regions continues to struggle with the broader mission we all have in nurturing and schooling students of color. Mentorship is an important piece in this struggle. Aspirations can be nurtured but how can cultural histories including multiple ways of knowing and living in the world also be addressed if at all? For instance, research demonstrates that when some Latino male students are only pushed into academic success, there are various tensions and frustrations that arise over their miseducation (Carrillo, 2016). Hence, the apolitical project, the mentorship moment primarily for access and the desire to "rise up," is layered with silences and even toxic possibilities. Those may not be the intentions of these efforts, but the core issue of potential toxicity remains.

We know that all pedagogy, even if well-intentioned, is layered with political dimensions and contradictions. This reality is inescapable. Even with its many successes, our evaluation of GM and the depth of this data confirms this political dimension and the importance of this critique. It is important to examine what we promote via our mentoring curriculum and ideology. This is part of the reflexive praxis that this book pursues and this part of what we offer to the reader in terms offering a conversation piece that pushes toward intentional programming that works to be additive, critical, and more inclusive of questions of power.

## References

Applebaum, B. (2010). *Being White, being good: White complicity, white moral responsibility, and social justice pedagogy*. Lanham, MD: Lexington Books.

Baker, D. B., & Maguire, C. P. (2005). Mentoring in historical perspective. In D. L. DuBois & M. J. Karcher (Eds.), *Handbook of youth mentoring* (pp. 14–29). Thousand Oaks, CA: Sage Publications.

Camangian, P. (2013). Seeing through lies: Teaching ideological literacy as a corrective lens. *Equity and Excellence in Education, 46*, 119–134.

Carrillo, J. F. (2013). I always knew i was gifted: Latino males and the Mestiz@ Theory of Intelligences (MTI). *Berkeley Review of Education, 4*(1), 69–95.

Carrillo, J. F. (2016). *Barrio nerds: Latino males, schooling, and the beautiful struggle*. Rotterdam, The Netherlands: Sense Publishers.

Deutsch, N. L., Lawrence, E. C., Henneberger, A. K. (2014). Social class. In D. L. DuBois & M. J. Karcher (Eds.), *Handbook of youth mentoring* (pp. 175–188). Thousand Oaks, CA: Sage Publications.

DuBois, D. L., & Karcher, M. J. (Eds.). (2013). *Handbook of youth mentoring*. Thousand Oaks, CA: Sage Publications.

Duncan-Andrade, J. M. R. (2009). Note to educators: Hope required when growing roses in concrete. *Harvard Educational Review, 79*, 181–194.

Freedman, M. (1993). *The kindness of strangers: Adult mentors, urban youth, and the new voluntarism*. San Francisco, CA: Jossey-Bass.

Freire, P. (1993). *Pedagogy of the oppressed*. New York, NY: Continuum.

Goldner, L., & Mayseless, O. (2009). The quality of mentoring relationships and mentoring success. *Journal of Youth and Adolescence, 38*(10), 1339.

Holland, D., Skinner, D., Lachicotte Jr., W., & Cain, C. (1998). *Identity in cultural worlds*. Cambridge, MA: Harvard University Press.

Liang, B., Bogat, G. A., & Duffy, N. (2013). Gender in mentoring relationships. In D. DuBois & M. Karcher (Eds.), *Handbook of youth mentoring* (2nd ed., pp. 159–174). Thousand Oaks, CA: Sage Publications.

Liou, D. D., Martinez, A. N., & Rotheran-Fuller, E. (2016). Don't give up on me: Critical mentoring pedagogy for the classroom building students' community cultural wealth. *International Journal of Qualitative Studies in Education, 29*(1), 104–129.

McDougall, M., & Beattie, R. S. (1997). Peer mentoring at work: the nature and outcomes of Nonhierarchical developmental relationships, *Management Learning, 28*, 423–437.

McGuire, G. M., & Reger, J. (2003). Feminist co-mentoring: A model for academic professional development. *National Women's Studies Journal, 15*(1), 54–72.

Moll, L. C., Amanti, C., Neff, D., & Gonzalez, N. (1992). Funds of knowledge for teaching: Using a qualitative approach to connect homes and classrooms. *Theory into Practice, 31*(2), 132–141.

Murry, A. (1778). *Mentoria: The young ladies instructor*. London: J. Fry & Co.

paperson, la. (2017). *A third university is possible*. Minneapolis, MN: University of Minnesota Press.

Sánchez, B., Colón-Torres, Y., Feuer, R., Roundfiled, K. E., & Berardi, L. (2005). Race, ethnicity, and culture in mentoring relationships. In D. L. DuBois & M. J. Karcher (Eds.), *Handbook of youth mentoring* (pp. 191–204). Thousand Oaks, CA: Sage Publications.

Schippers, M. (2008). Doing difference/doing power: Negotiations of race and gender in a mentoring program. *Symbolic Interaction, 31*, 77–98.

Tierney, J., & Grossman, J. (2000). What works in promoting positive youth development: Mentoring. In M. P. Kluger, G. Alexander, & P. Curtis (Eds.), *What works in child welfare* (pp. 323–328). Washington, DC: CWLA Press.

Yosso, T. J. (2005). Whose culture has capital? A critical race theory discussion of community cultural wealth. *Race, Ethnicity, and Education, 8*(1), 69–91.

CHAPTER 1

# Capitalizing on Achievement: A Critical Examination of School-Based Mentoring Programs and Student Achievement

*Shanyce L. Campbell*

## 1 Introduction

In today's global economy, productivity is highly dependent on the availability of knowledgeable and skilled workers. The shift to a knowledge-based economy has caused educational leaders and policymakers to focus on the college going of K-12 students, especially students of color, as a means of maintaining the United States' global and political competitiveness. Schools serve as institutions that fulfill the needs of society by preparing all students for labor market participation. However, schools nudge a select group of students into higher status positions by offering them access to a higher ordered curriculum (Davis & Moore, 1945). This opportunity hoarding mechanism produces unequal access to financial, social, cultural, and human capital, which create inequalities within and between schools (Massey, 2010). As schools face accountability pressures from No Child Left Behind and Race to the Top, to promote student achievement, the use of targeted services and programs such as school-based mentoring programs (SBM) have become a possible strategy to minimize the education debt of students of color.

Mentoring is often defined as a nonparental adult and student relationship where the nonparental adult seeks to foster a student's socio-emotional, cognitive and identity development (DuBois, Portillo Rhodes, Silverthorn, & Valentine, 2011; Thompson & Kelly-Vance, 2001). In general there are two types of mentoring relationships: natural mentoring and planned mentoring. Natural mentoring involves mentoring as a result of an existing friendship, social relationship (e.g., teaching and coaching); whereas, planned mentoring occurs systematically through structured programs (Thompson & Kelly-Vance, 2001).

The growth of planned mentoring programs stemmed from a comprehensive evaluation of the Big Brother/Big Sister of America (BBBSA), the largest and known mentoring organization in the United States. Tierney, Grossman, and Resch (1995) found that BBBSA had positive effects on substance abuse, school attendance, behavior and parental involvement. Despite the marginal

© KONINKLIJKE BRILL NV, LEIDEN, 2019 | DOI: 10.1163/9789004407985_002

effects, this report garnered support by policymakers and practitioners and lead to a proliferation and funding of mentoring programs across the country (Rhodes & DuBois, 2006; Wheeler, Keller, & DuBois, 2010). However, evaluations of mentoring programs show that these programs are not comprehensive in the effects on student outcomes. For instance, some evaluations suggest that mentoring have positive impacts on socio-emotional or identity development, but not student test performance (Wheeler, Keller, & DuBois, 2010). Other evaluation studies suggest that mentoring programs have positive effects on student test scores and grade point averages (Thompson & Kelly-Vance, 2001; DuBois et al., 2011).

This chapter critically examines the effect of school-based mentoring programs on increasing student achievement, as measured by standardized test scores through a mixed methods approach. Using quantitative data I will examine whether SBM has an effect on students' standardized test scores. Qualitative data will be used to supplement the quantitative results and provide a deeper understanding of how SBM programs incorporate academics into activities and discussions with students of color.

This study expands the research on mentoring programs through a rigorous and comprehensive design. As mentoring programs for students continue to be a major way schools, nonprofits, and communities improve outcomes for students, it is essential we understand how and why these programs are effective, if at all. In the next section, I discuss the theoretical framework for this study then briefly describe the mentoring program (Gold Medal) that is examined in this chapter. I then provide details on the qualitative and quantitative methods and findings. I conclude this chapter with a discussion of the findings and implications for mentoring programs, more broadly.

## 2 Theoretical Framework

The use of standardized tests to assess student achievement in this standards-based reform era and the subsequent use of deficit-based mentoring programs as solutions, I use social reproduction theory as the theoretical framework. More specifically, this essay examines students' acquisition of social and institutional and White cultural capital from mentor in efforts to understand whether these resources influence student achievement.

### 2.1 Social Capital and Student Achievement
Social capital owes its origins to the scholarship of Pierre Bourdieu in the 1980s. According to Bourdieu (1983), social capital is defined as "the aggregate of the

actual or potential resources that are linked to possession of a durable network of more or less institutionalized relationships of mutual acquaintance and recognition" (Bourdieu, 1983, pp. 102–103). According to Bourdieu, social relationships or networks allow individuals to access the resources possessed by other members. The size and quality of these relationships are salient factors that assist in acquiring social capital. Unlike human capital, which includes the knowledge and skills possessed by individuals, social capital provides a more robust set of resources, if by magnitude alone, because it is based on the relationships and resources between individuals. Together, social and human capital aide in increasing individual and societal economic capital.

However, contextual factors such as the economic structure, race relations, gender relations, et cetera, shape the interactions between members, which may grant opportunities to some and reproduce inequalities for others. In discussions of social capital and race, one focus is on the quantity of social ties. Some scholars suggest that people of color have fewer social networks than Whites (Martineau, 1977; Stanton-Salazar, 1997). While other scholars argue that because of the collectivist nature of people of color, these groups hold more social ties and rely on the ties more frequently than Whites who are often characterized as an individualistic group (MacPhee, Fritz, Miller-Heyl, 1996; Kohn & Wilson, 1995). There is also a similar debate across social capital and class (Cochran, 1993; Portes & Landolt, 1996; Lareau, 2003).

Much of the current literature on social capital in education focuses on parents, teachers, nonparental adults, peers, and extracurricular networks (Ream & Palardy, 2008; Stanton-Salazar, 1997; Stanton-Salazar & Dornbusch, 1995; Dika & Singh, 2002; Lareau & Horvat, 1999). These networks provide several sources of social capital such as advocacy, support/encouragement, immaterial resources (e.g., information) and material resources (e.g., supplies, transportation, written feedback, etc.), which foster pro-academic attitudes and behaviors.

The relationships and networks students establish within the school setting has the potential to influence academic performance. Some students seek out and interact with teachers and nonparental adults in ways that benefits them academically and non-academically such as leniency with grading, receiving additional academic support, receiving information regarding post-high school opportunities, and providing advice regarding romantic relationships. Yet disconnects between teachers and students may result in behavioral problems and low academic motivations.

Examining the presence of teacher-student relationships, Crosnoe, Johnson, and Elder (2004) found that across all students (race-gendered students), positive relationships with teachers were associated with increased academic performance. These results were especially salient among students attending private schools and schools where the racial and ethnic makeup was more reflective of the student's own race or ethnicity. The study also found that Latinas experienced the greatest positive effect from teacher bonding.

It is evident from the literature that counselors also hold a significant role in academic success or failure of students (Cicourel & Kitsuse, 1963; Ogbu, 2003; Riehl, Pallas, & Natriello, 1999). Stevens (2007) illustrates the importance of relationships between students and counselors, as counselors provided avenues of interaction with college representatives. In a study examining the role of social capital on college going among Latina students, González, Stoner, and Jovel (2003) found that counselors provided material and immaterial supports to students on college tracks and were influential in their university decision-making process. For students on the community college track, counselors were not influential in their decision-making and in some cases students were not in any contact with counselors.

Missing from the discussion of social capital at the K-12 level is the role of non-school related mentors in creating and maintaining social capital. There is some evidence at the post-secondary level that mentors help students of color navigate the educational process by providing students with knowledge about the academic culture (Smith, 2007). Researchers are also cautious not to claim that there is a strong correlation between mentoring and academic achievement because of the presence of other confounding factors (Hedges & Mania-Farnell, 2002).

Despite the limited research, we know that mentors often serve as institutional agents who promote educational attainment and behavioral development among students. According to Stanton-Salazar (2011), an institutional agent is defined as "an individual who occupies one or more hierarchical positions of relatively high-status and authority. Such an individual ... manifests his or her potential role ..., when, on behalf of the adolescent, he or she acts to directly transmit, or negotiate the transmission of highly valued resources ..." (p. 1067). For students of color, especially from low-income families, these agents or mentors provide students with beneficial opportunities and supports, such as assistance with college applications, tutoring, and developing weak ties with higher status individuals (Dreher & Cox, 1996, Smith, 2000). This social capital allows students to increase their human capital needed to succeed academically.

## 2.2 *Cultural Capital and Student Achievement*

Bourdieu and Passeron (1973) first used the concept cultural capital to understand how educational outcomes differed based on culture. Cultural capital

CAPITALIZING ON ACHIEVEMENT

refers to knowledge, skills, education and advantages that a person possesses. Much of the literature regarding cultural capital employs a deficit lens, where people of color are viewed as having little to no cultural capital, because this form of capital is understood as "societally valued knowledge of high-brow culture" (DiMaggio, 1982; Lareau & Weininger, 2003; Yosso, 2005; Roscigno & Ainsworth-Darnell, 1999, p. 153). High-brow activities include attending museums, participating in extracurricular activities in dance, art or music (DiMaggio, 1982). Not only do scholars take on this deficit view, educational institutions also function under the premise that celebrates White, middle-class cultural capital. Teachers as gatekeepers of cultural capital may reward White, middle class students who possess this *acceptable* form of capital rewarding them with more affirming teacher-student interactions. Students of color who are able to acquire this institutional, cultural capital have the ability to navigate these power structures and successfully "do school."

The literature on cultural capital and student achievement is scant. One study examining the relationship between race, cultural capital, and educational resources found that cultural classes (e.g., art, music, and dance) had a positive relationship on students' grade point average and standardized test scores (Roscigno & Ainsworth-Darnell, 1999). They also found that cultural trips (e.g., museums) had a positive relationship on standardized test scores.

## 3 Background of the Mentoring Program

The Gold Medal mentoring program is a district-wide support program aimed at improving the achievement of students of color. The program began almost 20 years ago under the recommendation from a task force created to improve African American student achievement through a school-community partnership. With the growing Hispanic and Burmese population in the district, the program also provides support for students from these ethnic groups. Over the past 16 years, the program has served more than 250 students.

During the study period, the program was funded primarily by private funds and the remaining support from the local district. Students are referred to mentorship program during the fourth grade by a school social worker based on three subjective characteristics of the students: (1) the presence of untapped potential; (2) the student seek out adult attention; and (3) the student's family agrees to be involved. Once a student is referred to the program, they must agree to stay in the program for the duration of their education career while in the district.

There are eight primary components of the program: mentoring, advocacy, tutoring, social and cultural enrichment, college and career preparation, parental involvement, scholarships and leadership development. However, the core feature of the program is the mentorship opportunity where during a student's fourth grade year will receive an adult community mentor. Mentors are required to undergo intense pre-service training, agree to commit to at least two years with a two-hour minimum per week commitment to their mentee and regularly report back to the organization regarding the activities and events the mentor and mentee have participated in. Irrespective of the two-year commitment, a large number stay with their original assigned students through high school completion. Unlike the traditional roles of mentors, the mentors in this program serve as mentor-advocates who provide or assist in providing educational supports for the students to ensure their academic success.

The district is located in a southeastern town. Overall, all student groups perform higher than the state average. All of the teachers are classified as "highly qualified" and most have over ten years of teaching experience. Despite, these positive outcomes, the districts principal turnover rate is higher than the state average, while the teacher turnover rate is on par with the state average.

## 4 Methodology

This essay employs a mixed methods design to understand how and why school-based mentoring programs affect student achievement. Mixed method research has grown over the past decade as a method for answering many complex, interdisciplinary social issues (Small, 2011). Consistent with other researchers, I used a complementary mixed methods approach, where interview (qualitative) data is used to interpret the results derived from a large quasi-experiment (quantitative) (Harding, 2009).

As illustrated in Figure 1.1, the impact of school-based mentoring programs on student achievement is guided by the following research questions:

1. Does participation in school-based mentoring programs increase student achievement, as measured by standardized test scores?
2. What is the role of mentors in improving students' test performance?

### 4.1 Quantitative Methods

#### 4.1.1 Data

The data for this study come from the district's testing and evaluation department administrative data on all students in the districts. The sample includes students from 14 of the 19 schools within the district over an eight year period (2002–2003 through 2010–2011). For these students, exam scores in mathematics, reading, algebra I, English I, biology, and U.S. history were collected. Over

CAPITALIZING ON ACHIEVEMENT    19

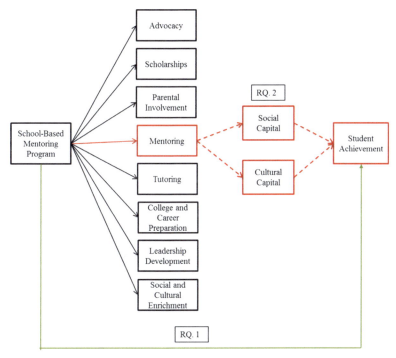

FIGURE 1.1   Conceptual framework

the study period, the students in the sample took approximately 38,000 exams; however, because of testing requirements and missing data cases were reduced.

### 4.1.2   Measures

#### 4.1.2.1   *Dependent Variable*

Beginning in third grade, students in North Carolina are required to take either an End-of-Grade (EOG) or End-of-Course (EOC) exam each year. These statewide exams are criterion-referenced multiple-choice tests used to assess student knowledge and skills in accord with the North Carolina Standard Course of Study. Test scores are standardized across grade and subject with a mean of zero and standard deviation of one to account for differences in the tests. As of the 2008–2009 academic year, 5th and 8th grade students are also required to take an EOG exam in science; however, this was not included in our analysis. Additionally, middle school students may also take the Algebra I EOC exam. At the high school level, students are required to take algebra I, English I, biology, and U.S. history EOC exams. As of the 2008–2009 school year, students were allowed to retake EOGs and EOCs. For this analysis, a student's highest score received on a given exam is considered.

#### 4.1.2.2 *Program Indicator*

The variable of interest for the evaluation of program effectiveness is a dichotomous variable that indicates students' participation in the mentoring program. The variable includes students who have *ever* participated in the mentoring program.

#### 4.1.2.3 *Student Characteristics*

A dichotomous variable was created to account for racial and ethnic differences in participation. Because there were no White program participants during the study years, the variable indicated whether a student was Black or a non-Black student of color. Non-Black students of color include: Hispanics, Native Americans, and Multiethnic/multiracial students. Eligibility for the free or reduced price lunch program was included as proxy for family resources. Free and reduced price lunch participation were combined into one dichotomous variable indicating whether the student was eligible for either service or ineligible. In addition, I include control variables for two exceptionality statuses: Academically and Intellectually Gifted (AIG) and students who have disabilities (SWD). A dichotomous variable for English language learners who are receiving services was included (ELL). As an indicator of absenteeism, I included the number of days a student was absent from school. Finally, I include a control for the gender of each student. Teacher, classroom, or school-level was not available for this analysis.

### 4.2 *Analytic Plan*

To assess the impact of the program on student achievement, a two-step approach that includes a measurement and analysis model are employed. Because I have no control over which students participate in program and which do not, therefore, in the measurement model I create a counterfactual group of those who do not participate in the program using propensity score matching. Propensity score matching is a technique, which uses a vector of observed variables to predict the probability that a student would be assigned the treatment group (Rosenbaum & Rubin, 1983).

Consistent with prior studies, propensity scores were estimated using a logistic regression model (Fan & Nowell, 2011). The estimated scores from the logistic regression analysis were then used to match participants and non-participants students. Several matching approaches currently exist in the literature; however, there is not a general consensus on the *best* approach to employ (Stuart, 2010; Baser, 2006; Austin, 2008; Rosenbaum & Rubin, 1984). In this study, I used the one nearest neighbor without replacement approach. This approach selects a program student and finds her/his closest non-program

CAPITALIZING ON ACHIEVEMENT

student match based on the propensity score. Without replacement, ensures that non-program student can only be matched to one program student. After the students are matched, equivalence between the samples from the treatment and control groups based on the observed controls was determined using t-tests. Once equivalence was determined, this sample was used to estimate the effect of program participation on student achievement.

The analysis estimating the effects of program participation on student achievement was conducted using the regression model shown in Equation (1):

$$Y_i = \beta_0 + \beta_1 T + \beta_2 Race/Ethnicity + \beta_3 EDS + \beta_4 AIG + \beta_5 SWD + \beta_6 ELL \qquad (1)$$
$$+ \beta_7 Days\ Absent + \beta_8 Gender + \varepsilon_i$$

where $Y_{igt}$ is the test score for student $i$; $\beta_1$ is the coefficient on the program indicator variable; and $\varepsilon i$ is the disturbance error.

## 4.3    *Results*

In answering the first research question on the impact of the program on student achievement, I find that participation in the mentorship program does not have a statistically significant effect on student test score performance. Although there are no statistically significant findings, it is important to note the direction of the effects. The coefficient of mentorship program is positive in the math, middle school algebra I, and English I models. Subsequently, the coefficient of the program is negative in the reading, high school algebra I, biology and U.S. history models.

The relationship between student-level characteristics and achievement was consistent with prior research. For example, students identified as AIG scored significantly higher than their peers, whereas, students with SWD scored lower than their peers. School attendance was positively related to student achievement. In the math model, boys scored higher than girls; however, in the English I model, girls scored significantly higher than boys. Black students scored lower than non-Black students of color in English I and biology.

The non-significant results from the quantitative analysis called into question reasons for the lack of impact of the program on student test score performance. Statistically, the small treatment sample size, which may produce less precise estimate of the treatment effect. Despite the statistical limitations, another weakness of this design is its ability to provide a more in-depth analysis of the reasons for the findings. Here I supplement the regression results, by examining interviews conducted by the evaluation team to understand what contributions mentors have on increasing student achievement for students participating in school-based mentoring programs?

TABLE 1.1    Characteristics of Mentors

| Mentor[a] | Race/Gender | Years mentoring | Mentor's profession | Completed post-secondary education | Mentor-mentee racial/ethnic congruence |
|---|---|---|---|---|---|
| Dominique | Black female | 1 | Unknown | Yes | Same race |
| John | White male | 1 | University professor | Yes | Cross race |
| Michael | White male | 2 | Doctoral student | Yes | Cross race |
| Jose[b] | White-Hispanic male | 2 | Retired financial banker | Yes | Semi-cross race |
| Barbara | White female | 2 | Unknown | Yes | Cross race |
| Miriam | White female | 2 | Lawyer | Yes | Cross race |
| Robin | Black female | 3 | Unknown | Yes | Same race |
| Susan | Hispanic female | 3.5 | Retired court reporter | Yes | Cross race |
| Lamont | Black male | 4 | Teacher | Yes | Same race |
| Lisa | White female | 6 | Social worker | Yes | Cross race |
| Wendy | White female | 7 | Entrepreneur | Yes | Cross race |
| Mariana[c] | Hispanic female | 2 0.5 | Educator | Yes | Same race |
| Charles[d] | White male | 6 0.5 | Retired economic developer | Yes | Cross race |

a  Pseudonyms are used for all mentors.
b  Jose's race is White and ethnicity is Hispanic.
c  Mariana currently has two same-race mentees.
d  Charles currently has two cross-race mentees.

### 4.4    *Qualitative Methods*

#### 4.4.1    Data Collection

As previously mentioned, the data was drawn from a larger evaluation that included 10 observations of program activities and a total of 76 interviews from mentees (former and current), parents of the mentees, the mentors, and the program staff during 2012. Because I focus specifically on the contributions of mentors, only interviews by the mentors are included in the analysis.

CAPITALIZING ON ACHIEVEMENT

TABLE 1.2    Descriptive statistics on mentors

| | |
|---|---|
| Percent male | 46% |
| Percent female | 62% |
| Percent Black | 23% |
| Percent White | 62% |
| Percent Hispanic | 8% |
| Percent biracial | 8% |
| Percent cross race | 62% |
| Percent same race[a] | 38% |
| Percent college graduates | 100% |
| Average years mentoring | 3.47 |
| | (0.5–8 years)[b] |
| $N = 13$ | |

a  The multiracial mentor was included in this percentage.

b  Refers to the range of years mentoring.

Semi-structured interviews were used to allow for possible probing. Mentors were asked to respond to questions about mentees' family background, mentor-mentee relationship, impact of race in the mentee-mentor relationship, networks, advocacy and mentees' goals. Interviews lasted from approximately 18 minutes up to 56 minutes.

### 4.4.2    Sample Selection

Thirteen mentor interviews was used in the analysis. Table 1.2 provides characteristics of the mentors in my sample. In the sample, the majority of the mentors were White, 38% White women and 23% White men. On average, volunteers served as mentors with their current mentees for 2.8 years. At the time of the interview, some mentors had recently been matched to their mentee and had only served for several months whereas others served as a mentor for up to eight years. The majority (62%) of the mentor-mentee matches were cross-race. All mentors completed post-secondary education. There were two mentors that currently have two mentees; all other mentors had a single student.

### 4.5    *Analysis*

The interviews were transcribed and entered into a qualitative analysis software program, Atlas.ti. These data were coded, and analyzed for themes related to social, cultural, human capital acquisition other themes that inductively emerged in the analysis. The analytic procedure involves several phases including organizing data, generating categories and themes, coding of the data (Marshall & Rossman, 2006). Each transcription was read several times in order ensure immersion and familiarity of the data. Patterns expressed by mentors were noted to themes. Codes were also arranged in clusters based on racial/ethnic congruence between mentors and mentees to detect systematic differences by.

## 5    Findings

The findings in this section are organized first by the broader social and cultural capital frameworks. Findings derived from the themes under each of these frameworks are discussed.

### 5.1    *Social Capital*

In this analysis, mentees acquired social capital from their mentors primarily through networks and connections and academic supports.

### 5.1.1    Networks and Connections

Across the interviews, mentors discussed the importance of serving as a bridging agent and institutional broker to introduce students to influential professions (Stanton-Salazar, 2011). The networks that mentors provided access to was both racially and ethnically different and similar than the mentee's race or ethnicity. Among the racially and ethnically different networks, mentors introduced their mentees to high-status individuals for several reasons, including employment opportunities and learning about potential career paths. For example, Susan a mentor states,

> I am blessed to live in an area over here ... that has many professionals ... I set something up and we go and talk to doctors, psychologists, social workers, um there's a guy that's a professor of Sociology ... she audited [his] class yesterday. She met, um ... the head [of a department on a university campus] ... Anytime I have an opportunity for someone that has an occupation that I thought that she didn't know about ...

In addition to racially incongruent networking relationships, mentors also introduced to mentors to individuals who "looked like them." Regardless of the mentor's race or ethnicity, mentors are very intentional about connecting their mentees with professionals of color. These mentors wanted send the message that despite harmful societal stereotypes, there are successful professionals of color. Obviously, this message was more fluid for mentors of color, who not only connected their mentees with professionals of color by happenstance (i.e., they were more likely to have friends of color), but also served as a racially or ethnically similar connection. For instance, Lamont, a same-race mentor, emphasizes.

> I think as an African American male, um, who has been successful in school and things like that, I would hope that, um, that's been helpful for [my mentee] to see that you can be intelligent and be black and be a male and still enjoy sports and all those different things.

John, cross-race mentor, states:

> He [mentee] met a friend of mine who's, um, Black and is a fellow who has his Ph.D. He's from Texas from a rural areas, grew up uh in poverty and he likes to says he was one of the families in town that know when to take a bath you had to go outside. So this friend of mine who is also a colleague has a very successful in a nonprofit here in [the town] so it's good that they had a chance to meet.

Not only did some mentors seek out people of color to introduce to their mentee, some also sought after cultural opportunities. One mentor who had not found a person of color to introduce her mentee states:

> I would love to find some Latino pediatricians to introduce her to and to talk with. I would really love to find someone who has been in her situation, you know, who's been, um, an extremely intelligent, poor, undocumented immigrant and has been able to overcome that to, you know, pursue their dreams. I'd love for her to be ... to see some people in her shoes that have done it. I don't know where they are. But I'd love to find them.

To summarize, networks and connections are valuable sources of social capital. Although networks and connections did not appear to directly influence academic outcomes, these networks serve as motivating factors for students to strive to achieve academically. Moreover, regardless of the mentor-mentee racial or ethnic congruence, mentors felt that introducing students of color to mentors of their same race or ethnicity was important in dismantling the notion that people of color are not successful educationally and professionally.

### 5.1.2 Academic Supports

Across the interviews, none of the mentors discussed the statewide standardized tests student are required to take each year. The only discussion around standardized testing occurred when Barbara, discussed helping her mentee with SAT prep.

> Well, we do .... I try to do a combination of stuff. Now that she has been cramming for SATs and things like that, we spend a lot more time doing practice SAT stuff and we talk through it and we go through the problems together. I talk to her about strategies and we have worked on vocabulary. But all along, we have always read and she had a lot of trouble reading when we met and she was not a good reader at all. And I just kept it up and we found a lot of books that she liked to read.

Much of the references to academic performance centered on the mentees grades across classes and subjects. When mentees struggled academically, mentors would tutor the student, put the student in touch with after school programs, or allow the mentorship program to handle the academic issues through its tutoring services. Mentors commented:

> I spent a fair amount of time one summer tutoring him in math though I don't see that as a mentor's mission. I'm hoping that he ... gets up to grade level within a year or so. ... I have talked to [the mentee's] teachers and said look if there is a problem you let me know. I borrowed a book from the school, to do the tutoring.
>
> But right now [the mentorship program] has got a tutor for her that is meeting with her twice a week just individual tutoring in math, which I think is unbelievable ... and she feels like she is really catching up.

Mentors also discussed the importance of their mentee reading and would incorporate this into their time spent together, which has been shown to positively affect academic performance (Robinson & Harris, 2014). For example, Miriam, a cross-race mentor, states:

> And [the mentee] doesn't like to read. So part of our relationship has been me trying to get her to read, and my daughter the middle school teacher has been giving us books and we actually found a series she likes, so we're glad for that

Another mentor states:

> We go to the [public library] and um she would pick out a book, we would go to a quiet corner; she would read to me.

CAPITALIZING ON ACHIEVEMENT

Susan, a cross-race, mentor used reading as a way to improve her mentee's language skills. She states:

> I would say the one thing that I work with her on more than probably anyone, because I do speak perfect English and I'm around her often is I working on her language skills. I have her read to me often. I tell her that if, you know, she come stop a word and she doesn't know what it means, even if she doesn't know it as a stop for her she needs to stop. I bought her a little dictionary. You need to look up that word and understand at least basically what that world means so you can go on.

To summarize, no mentor mentioned the statewide standardized test that students must take each year. What seemed to be most important were letter grades, which supports the positive correlation between the mentor program and grade point average found in a previous evaluation of this program. Although, there were no significant results in terms of reading test scores, it is clear that mentors paid much attention to reading with their mentees.

## 5.2    *Cultural Capital*

The analysis of the data suggests that cultural capital was acquired by exposure to new experiences, language correction, and development of social norms. The activities mentees were exposed to varied by financial cost and normed social status. Table 1.3 provides a list of the activities that took place between the mentor and mentee. Among the activities listed, there is only one that is directly related to academics—attending and participating in a science fair. Only two other activities were tangentially related to academics, college tours and visiting the library.

### 5.2.1    Exposure and Opportunities

Providing mentees with experiences and exposures to things they may have otherwise not experienced was a key theme in this analysis. Same-race mentors often discussed the lack of exposure to things in their own lives growing up and using this mentoring relationship as an opportunity to give back by exposing their mentees to other experiences. Cross-race mentors often discussed providing exposure to activities and events because parents did not have the means financially. This often came across in a manner that could be interpreted as cross-race mentors possessing a savior mentality when they did take mentees to events.

TABLE 1.3   Mentor-mentee activities

| Financially costly activities | Financially inexpensive activities |
| --- | --- |
| *Arts* | |
| Ballet | Festivals |
| Alvin Ailey dance performance | Crafts |
| Museums | |
| Circus (including Cirque du Soleil) | |
| Sewing camp | |
| *Outdoors* | |
| Skiing | Swimming |
| Visiting mentor's assistant's horse | Hiking |
| Gardens (Duke Gardens & Botanical Gardens) | Fishing |
| Canoeing | Camping |
| Airplane flying | |
| Built a chicken coup | |
| Rafting | |
| Walking mentor's donkey | |
| *Educational* | |
| Science fair | Visiting the Library |
| College visits (local) | |
| *Vacation Trips* | |
| Disney | |
| Beach | |
| | *Games* |
| | Playing Board or Video games |
| | (Yahtzee, Monopoly, & Scrabble) |
| | Basketball |
| | Soccer games |
| | Bowling |
| | Baseball |
| | *Cultural* |
| | Religious ceremonies (Buddhism, |
| | Catholicism, Judaism, & Christianity) |

(*cont.*)

CAPITALIZING ON ACHIEVEMENT

TABLE 1.3    Mentor-mentee activities (*cont.*)

| Financially costly activities | Financially inexpensive activities |
| --- | --- |
| | *Other* |
| | Hanging out at home |
| | Going out to eat |
| | Cooking at home |
| | Volunteer at animal shelters |
| | Going to the movie theatre |
| | Shopping at the mall |

Dominique, a same-race mentor, states:

> I want to bring exposure to her, um, just to see that there's more out there. I wish when I was growing up I had a mentor, um, just to kind of show me what I was missing. I feel like I didn't get exposed to a lot of things until later on in high school or when I was in college and I feel like as a child there was a lot that I missed out on because I didn't have … not to say my mom didn't want to, but she didn't have the time to exposure me to a lot of things …

Marianna another same-race mentor states:

> We have the experiences of having had grown up here and knowing that [this town] can be a bubble and trying to encourage them to go out of their comfort zone and how them that there is a bigger world out there even though my world was only extended to both sides of [this state].

Parents played an active role in exposing students to different educationally experiences. In discussing her mentee, who is from a single parent home, Marianna says:

> … [the mentee's family] went to Washington D.C. for the Dream Act … so you know it's just that networking that her mom has done in the community has opened up that door for Rosie go and see that.

Other mentors believed they were providing opportunities to mentees that the mentee's families were unable to provide.

So I do try to find new things for Angelica and I to do together so that she's, um, getting some inspiration from life ... things that maybe she wouldn't be introduced to from her family.

### 5.2.2 Language Correction

Linguistic differences between mentors and mentees play a significant role in acquiring "high-status" cultural capital. In efforts to achieve this acquisition of capital, mentors focused on mentees' linguistic communication style. However, this increased attention was often rooted in deficit ideologies surrounding language differences. Mentors assumed the responsibility of correcting or "improving" their mentees grammar to conform to North American English. In the analysis, only cross-race mentors mentioned correcting a mentees grammar. For instance, John, a cross-race mentor, states:

> ... I do find myself looking for opportunities to correct his language when we're talking together and he uses languages that isn't formally grammatical, uh, or you know sort of, significant non-standard pronunciation. I don't' usually correct him when it's just a matter of pronunciation or even sort of you know casual speech but if it's something outstanding or you know particulate if it's sort of an attempt to make sort of a more formal comment but he uses less formal language then I correct him. I guess I'd like him to recognize that class and race and social settings play a big role in language ... it's ok to use different forms of language but to sort of recognize when you use different forms of language ...

### 5.2.3 Development of Social Norms

Mentors used networking opportunities to teach mentees social norms regarding how to greet professionals and other adults. Mentors often instructed mentees about how to position their bodies and specific language to use when introducing themselves. Susan, who is very connected to the local community and a cross-race mentor, told her mentee, "when I introduce you ... eye contact, 'how do you do? It's nice to meet you.' It's not just the head down and we don't acknowledge the person." John, a cross-race mentor, also shares

> I hope I helped in small ways like when he meets with adults, he's not sure how to greet them. I've said, Tyrek when you meet somebody I say you know shake their hand say it's a pleasure to meet you Mr. so and so or Mrs. So and do, my name is you know ...

CAPITALIZING ON ACHIEVEMENT

In addition to sharing how to greet professionals, mentors also helped mentees navigate education system's cultural norms. Wendy, a cross-race mentor, states:

> One of the things I like doing with Isabella is explaining to her how the world works. You know, times when she has been infuriated in her classes, I have said 'if the teacher believes that you are interested in what's going on then she is going to cut you more slack than if you act out.

To summarize, three major themes were present in the discussion of cultural capital—exposure and opportunities, language correction, and the development of social norms. These themes are all beneficial to function in society; however, it is unclear whether these translate into better academic outcomes among the mentees. As one mentor states "... I really try to make them learn something new even if it's not academic." There are several indirect ways in which these themes affect academic achievement. For example, the exposure to certain activities may increase the mentees motivation to perform well in school in order to continue to participate in these activities with their mentors. Through mentors' correcting mentees' language, mentees could learn code-switching techniques, which are valuable in moving in and out of White spaces. Finally, the development of social norms also aids in teaching students behaviors that society deems as evidence of a "good citizen."

## 6     Discussion and Implications

In the current outcomes-based education reform system, programs receiving funding from federal and/or state governments are being pressured to show results, which often means increased test performance among the targeted group. With millions being spent on mentoring programs, if results do not move in the direction policymakers hope funding for many of these programs may be cut similar to the U.S. Department of Education's Student Mentoring Program Educators (Office of Management and Budget, 2009). The politics of education ties the hands of many mentoring programs if the focus is solely on test scores. As policymakers and educational leaders, continue the quest to improve education for all students, it is imperative that measures be appropriate, realistic, and evidence-based.

In this study, I examine the impact of mentoring on the academic achievement of students of color in a high performing, predominately White school district. Findings from the quantitative study show no effect of the mentorship program on students' standardized test scores, which is consistent with prior studies. To explore why there is no statistically significant relationship between mentoring programs and student test performance, I triangulate the administrative data with interviews from the mentors.

There are numerous studies that show that standardized test questions are culturally and economically bias toward white, middle-class families (Jencks, 1998; Harlow, 2011). These tests often use examples of activities and events unfamiliar to students of color and/or economically marginalized students. One of the underlying hypotheses from the qualitative study is that through mentoring relationship, students of color expand their knowledge and understanding of white cultural capital that tests are often created from.

The analysis of the interviews shows that mentors are not employing their own social or cultural capital in ways to directly improve test performance such as providing test-taking strategies. Instead, mentors provide mentees with social and cultural capital to navigate the larger society and indirectly impact test score performance.

As it relates to social capital and student achievement, one salient finding from this study is the attention mentors paid to reading. Mentors served as a connection who took mentees to the library and worked with mentees on their reading. While these efforts are related to positive academic outcomes, it is unclear the frequency of these activities among the mentor and mentee. Many of the activities were social in nature and not directly offering educational learning experiences. Additionally, mentors embraced the stereotypical perceptions regarding individuals of color and projected those onto mentees. For instance, mentors regardless of race or ethnicity connected students to same-race professionals to debunk the myths that people of color are unintelligent, uneducated, and are not professionals.

Turning to cultural capital, many of the White mentors took a superiority complex in transmitting cultural capital. The mentors failed to embrace the idea of difference, especially as it relates to linguistics, and held the position that standard White English was *the right* way to speak. This lack of regard for other forms of English is problematic and calls into question other aspects of the mentor-mentee relationship that may cause mentors to hold negative judgments about students of color home life, cultural backgrounds, et cetera. The superiority complex was also revealed in how mentors taught social norms such as greeting adults. There appeared to be no recognition of cultural differences in how mentees were to communicate with adults that research has shown to exist (Lareau, 2003). Mentors took an approach that suggests, "here's the right way" to greet people.

In the larger context, these White norms may prove to be beneficial in teaching students of color how to navigate through majority White spaces—school and society, but at a significant identify and emotional cost. Interestingly, this mentorship program requires an intense training that includes reading and discussing several scholarly texts related to social justice. However, it is unclear whether there is a lack of reflection among mentors, a lack of rigor in the training and discussion, or a combination of both.

The findings from this study suggest several directions for future research. First, studies should place increased attention on the impact of mentoring on non-test score outcomes such as socio-emotional, identity, and motivation to more deeply understand the benefits or consequences of mentoring programs. Second, a study on how mentees use social and cultural capital from mentors to benefit them academically, economically, and socially. Finally, future studies could examine the dosage of mentoring programs to capture whether mentoring or some other programmatic component drives the results on student outcomes.

### References

Austin, P. C. (2008). The performance of different propensity-score methods for estimating relative risks. *Journal of Clinical Epidemiology, 61*(6), 537–545.

Bourdieu, P. (1973). Cultural reproduction and social reproduction. In R. Brown (Ed.), *Knowledge, education, and cultural change* (pp. 71–84). London: Tavistock Publications.

Bourdieu, P. (1983). The field of cultural production: The economic world reversed. *Poetics, 12*(4), 311–356.

Cicourel, A. V., & Kitsuse, J. I. (1971). *The social organization of the high school and deviant adolescent careers. School and society: A sociological reader* (Prepared by the School and Society Course Team at The Open University). London: Routledge and Kegan Paul and Open University Press.

Cochran, M. (1993). Parenting and personal social networks. In T. Luster & L. Okagaki (Eds.), *Parenting: An ecological perspective* (pp. 149–178). Mahwah, NJ: Erlbaum.

Crosnoe, R., Johnson, M. K., & Elder, G. H. (2004). Intergenerational bonding in school: The behavioral and contextual correlates of student-teacher relationships. *Sociology of Education, 77*(1), 60–81.

Davis, K., & Moore, W. E. (1945). Some principles of stratification. *American Sociological Review, 10*, 242–249.

Dika, S. L., & Singh, K. (2002). Applications of social capital in educational literature: A critical synthesis. *Review of Educational Research, 72*(1), 31–60.

DiMaggio, P. (1982). Cultural capital and school success: The impact of status culture participation on the grades of US high school students. *American Sociological Review, 47*, 189–201.

Dreher, G. F., & Cox Jr., T. H. (1996). Race, gender, and opportunity: A study of compensation attainment and the establishment of mentoring relationships. *Journal of Applied Psychology, 81*(3), 297.

DuBois, D. L., Portillo, N., Rhodes, J. E., Silverthorn, N., & Valentine, J. C. (2011). How effective are mentoring programs for youth? A systematic assessment of the evidence. *Psychological Science in the Public Interest, 12*(2), 57–91.

Fan, X., & Nowell, D. L. (2011). Using propensity score matching in educational research. *Gifted Child Quarterly, 55*(1), 74–79.

Gonzalez, K. P., Stoner, C., & Jovel, J. E. (2003). Examining the role of social capital in access to college for Latinas: Toward a college opportunity framework. *Journal of Hispanic Higher Education, 2*(2), 146–170.

Harding, D. J. (2009). Violence, older peers, and the socialization of adolescent boys in disadvantaged neighborhoods. *American Sociological Review, 74*(3), 445–464.

Harlow, S. C. (2011). *Item fairness of the nonverbal subtests of the Stanford-Binet intelligence test, in a Latina.* Retrieved from ProQuest Dissertations & Theses Global. (Order No. 3485301)

Hill, N. E., & Tyson, D. F. (2009). Parental involvement in middle school: A meta-analytic assessment of the strategies that promote achievement. *Developmental Psychology, 45*(3), 740.

Hedges, K., & Mania-Farnell, B. (2002). Mentoring students in an introductory science course. *Journal of College Science Teaching, 32*(3), 194–198.

Jencks, C., & Phillips, M. (Eds.). (1998). *The Black-White test score gap.* Washington, DC: Brookings Institution Press.

Kohn, L. P., & Wilson, M. N. (1995). Social support networks in the African American family: Utility for culturally compatible intervention. *New Directions for Child and Adolescent Development, 1995*(68), 35–58.

Lareau, A. (2003). *Unequal childhoods: Race, class and family life.* Berkeley, CA: University of California Press.

Lareau, A., & Horvat, E. M. (1999). Moments of social inclusion and exclusion race, class, and cultural capital in family-school relationships. *Sociology of Education, 72*(1), 37–53.

Lareau, A., & Weininger, E. B. (2003). Cultural capital in educational research: A critical assessment. *Theory and Society, 32*(5–6), 567–606.

MacPhee, D., Fritz, J., & Miller-Heyl, J. (1996). Ethnic variations in personal social networks and parenting. *Child Development, 67*(6), 3278–3295.

Marshall, C., & Rossman, G. B. (2010). *Designing qualitative research* (5th ed.). Thousand Oaks, CA: Sage Publications.

Martineau, W. H. (1977). Informal social ties among urban Black Americans: Some new data and a review of the problem. *Journal of Black Studies, 8*(6), 83–104.

Ogbu, J. U. (2003). *Black American students in an affluent suburb: A study of academic disengagement.* New York, NY: Routledge.

Portes, A., & Landolt, P. (1996). The downside of social capital. *The American Prospect, 26*(94), 18–21.

Ream, R. K., & Palardy, G. J. (2008). Reexamining social class differences in the availability and the educational utility of parental social capital. *American Educational Research Journal, 45*(2), 238–273.

Rhodes, J. E., & DuBois, D. L. (2006). Understanding and facilitating the youth mentoring movement. *Social Policy Report, 22*(3), 3–20.

Riehl, C., Pallas, A. M., & Natriello, G. (1999). Rites and wrongs: Institutional explanations for the student course-scheduling process in urban high schools. *American Journal of Education, 107*(2), 116–154.

Robinson, K., & Harris, A. L. (2014). *The broken compass: Parental involvement with children's education.* Cambridge, MA: Harvard University Press.

Roscigno, V. J., & Ainsworth-Darnell, J. W. (1999). Race, cultural capital, and educational resources: Persistent inequalities and achievement returns. *Sociology of Education, 72*(3), 158–178.

Rosenbaum, P. R., & Rubin, D. B. (1984). Reducing bias in observational studies using subclassification on the propensity score. *Journal of the American Statistical Association, 79*(387), 516–524.

Small, M. L. (2011). How to conduct a mixed methods study: Recent trends in a rapidly growing literature. *Sociology, 37*(1), 57.

Smith, B. (2007). Accessing social capital through the academic mentoring process. *Equity & Excellence in Education, 40*(1), 36–46.

Smith, S. S. (2000). Mobilizing social resources: Race, ethnic, and gender differences in social capital and persisting wage inequalities. *The Sociological Quarterly, 41*(4), 509–537.

Stanton-Salazar, R. D. (1997). A social capital framework for understanding the socialization of racial minority children and youths. *Harvard Educational Review, 67*(1), 1–41.

Stanton-Salazar, R. D., & Dornbusch, S. M. (1995). Social capital and the reproduction of inequality: Information networks among Mexican-origin high school students. *Sociology of Education, 68*(2), 116–135.

Stuart, E. A. (2010). Matching methods for causal inference: A review and a look forward. *Statistical Science: A Review Journal of the Institute of Mathematical Statistics, 25*(1), 1.

Thompson, L. A., & Kelly-Vance, L. (2001). The impact of mentoring on academic achievement of at-risk youth. *Children and Youth Services Review, 23*(3), 227–242.

Tierney, J. P., Grossman, J. B., & Resch, N. L. (1995). *Making a difference: An impact study of big brothers/big sisters.* Philadelphia, PA: Public/Private Ventures.

Wheeler, M. E., Keller, T. E., & DuBois, D. L. (2010). Review of three recent randomized trials of school-based mentoring: Making sense of mixed findings. *Social Policy Report, 24*(3), 3–21.

Yosso, T. J. (2005). Whose culture has capital? A critical race theory discussion of community cultural wealth. *Race, Ethnicity, and Education, 8*(1), 69–91.

CHAPTER 2

# Someone Fabulous Like Me: White Mentors' Representations of Moralities and Possibilities for a White Complicity Pedagogy for Mentoring

*Amy Senta and Danielle Parker Moore*

## 1    Introduction

The purpose of this chapter is to examine White mentors' representations of moralities to the research team evaluating their mentoring program. The mentoring program brought White adults and youth of color into a relationship as "mentors" and "mentees." Much of the work aiming for anti-racist education situates cross-race relationships as an important site of investigation, and through this project we have become committed to a study that will contribute to the understandings of cross-race relationships. Furthermore, because the mentoring program aimed to create anti-racist relationships and Whiteness is a topic not yet explored in the field of mentoring studies, we aim to offer an interpretation of the experiences and perspectives of mentors involved in cross-race relationships to the field of mentoring studies. Finally, in describing White mentors' representations we also aim to contribute to the primarily theoretical work on White complicity.

## 2    Theoretical Framework

In order to come to interpretations that might contribute to these fields, we engage Applebaum's (2007) theory of morality. According to Applebaum, dominant conceptions of morality are based in the modern idea of individual autonomy, but a different morality based in a socially constructed subjectivity is necessary for Whites to take up a focus on complicity as well as potentially engage in anti-racist relationships. Applebaum has argued that recognition of complicity in racism, and therefore this new notion of moral responsibility, is a necessary condition for Whites' engagement in anti-racist relationships. This view involves subjectivity as constructed but not determined, so agency, like structure, is always at play. In this work, we ask what moralities

© KONINKLIJKE BRILL NV, LEIDEN, 2019 | DOI: 10.1163/9789004407985_003

are represented to be at play, and what those moralities might say about complicity.

As Applebaum (2010) did, we define Whiteness as a location of race privilege and structural advantage. Applebaum's notion of White complicity is based on this definition of Whiteness; all White individuals are explicitly responsible for racism because systems of racism benefit them. Applebaum (2010) wrote, "[A]ll Whites, by virtue of systemic White privilege that is inseparable from White ways of being, are implicated in the production and reproduction of systemic racial injustice" (p. 179). Because previous definitions of complicity were limited to complicity of the marginalized in their own marginalization, the notion of White complicity added complicity of the privileged to scholarship on complicity. Applebaum (2010) called for research that might add to the primarily theoretical notion of White complicity within the field of Whiteness studies. We argue that the representations from the White mentors involved in this study of a mentoring program can offer some understanding of their cross-race mentoring relationships which could present possibilities for White complicity pedagogy and Whiteness studies.

## 3 Methods of Analysis

We examined data in representations from twelve White mentors for perspectives on White complicity and moralities. Data included individual evaluation interviews on topics such as their mentoring history, relationships, and life stories. Data also included program files containing applications, initial match screening interviews, and activity logs.

Applebaum wrote that traditional notions of moral responsibility center Whites' attention on what they as individuals might do instead of on what might need to be done. The centering of the individual as an agent of change, according to Applebaum, leads to individualist phenomena such as White narcissism and heroism, and these phenomena center the White subject as authority, change agent, and as positioned away from that which is to be changed. Applebaum described this notion of responsibility to involve the concepts of causality, control, knowledge, choice, and intentions. Therefore, we deductively coded the data for indicators of these concepts.

Applebaum called for a rearticulated notion of moral responsibility that moves away from these individualist phenomena and towards uncertainty, vulnerability, and vigilance for White denials of complicity. Therefore, we deductively coded the data for indicators of these concepts as well.

## 4    Interpretations

We interpreted a perspective of objectivity in claims of ability to enact change as individuals. This perspective was based on modern ideas of autonomy, which was an assumption that seemed to prevent the mentors from considering their subjectivities to be socially constructed. Even though some described themselves to have no influence on the world through the mentoring relationships, sometimes even attributing racism to structural factors, the mentors' claims still seemed to be based in objectivity, as if the lack of influence were an individual failure. They may not have been able to act with Applebaum's notion of moral responsibility because moral agency did not emerge from a new subjectivity of White complicity.

## 5    Individual Agency

Mentors' representations seemed to be based on objectivity. They described their mentoring to involve their individual agency and for them, this individual agency occurred through relationships of causality. One mentor said, "I really believe that small, personal interventions make the biggest difference in society." This comment represents the most general sense of the mentors' description of the mentoring.

Views of individual agency through the mentoring seemed to involve a sense of moral heroism. One mentor, for example, called herself a "shepherd." We interpreted this sense of heroism through Applebaum's theoretical lens of moralities and came to an understanding of the mentors' representations of moralities being based on what Applebaum described as the traditional notion of moral responsibility. Mentors described a sense of control over the causal relationships involved in their individual agency.

The mentors often named a desire to "give" as their primary reason for becoming a mentor. This giving took many forms of individual agency in the mentors' representations but always involved a sense of moral heroism. One mentor said her mentee did not like to read, so the mentor spent their time together trying to get the mentee to read and fulfilling food bribes for reading quantities of pages. She described this pattern as successful. Another mentor was proud that she had taught her mentee to cook because she had caused her mentee to become "smart and capable," "careful," and "focused."

Forms of individual agency often seemed to be laced with a high degree of desire for control. One mentor, in particular, exemplified this desire for control. Finding existing grade reports to be lacking, the mentor hoped to design

SOMEONE FABULOUS LIKE ME

an additional progress report that would be submitted by the mentee's teachers directly to the mentor. The mentor had an existing scheme in place in which the mentor attached positive and negative monetary values to school grades and paid the mentee according to this scheme. Furthermore, the mentor argued that the mentoring program should set up face-to-face meetings for the mentors in which various people in each mentee's life, including tutors, family, and teachers, were brought together for each mentor. The mentors' desire for control seemed to us to also indicate a sense of mentor-centering. This mentor-centering reflects the centering of self often performed by Whites.

Taking a closer look at representations of what the mentors described as moral "giving" led us to two variations of forms of agency. These two variations, influencing other individuals in a mentee's life and influencing the mentee, strengthened our interpretation that the mentors approached their mentoring with a sense of individual agency through causality.

First, in many cases, the mentors represented individual agency in the form of influencing another person's individual agency. For example, mentors described cases in which they perceived themselves to have influenced the individual actions of individuals in the mentees' lives such as school counselors, teachers, or parents. For example, one mentor critiqued and interfered with a school counselor's decision to place a bilingual mentee in an English course that met online during the summer instead of a better course that met in person. Another mentor attributed her influence on others' agency to the capital she had acquired through her years involved in district administration, saying, "I sort of understand how the schools work and I have no trouble picking up the phone and calling somebody if I think I need to, or sending an email. I'm not intimidated by the schools. I feel really comfortable in that arena." She even expressed that this was the primary thing she brought to her relationship with the mentee.

In addition to representing hopes for influencing the individual agency of individuals in the mentees' lives, the mentors represented hopes for their agency to have influence on the future individual agency of their mentees. However, the ends of the imagined agency involved changing the mentees plans, for example, regarding their career goals. One mentor hoped to influence the mentee to abandon her goal of becoming a designer and instead work with "a lot more focus and direction" towards a career in the biological sciences. One mentor who thought her mentee was already "on a really, really good path" imagined her role as a mentor to be helping her stay on that path. Another mentor imagined that the mentee's family viewed her role as "keeping her on the right path" and preventing the mentee from "losing her way" as her mother had in her own youth.

## 6      Individual Agency and Race

The mentors seemed to have a sense of individual agency around the topic of race. One mentor said that his Black mentee sometimes told the mentor stories of oppression from the mentee's life while telling the mentor that the mentor wouldn't understand because the mentor was White. The mentor responded in these cases by denying his Whiteness to his mentee. The mentor told the mentee that although he had never seen a brown person until he traveled internationally and he "thought the whole world was just White people," he "grew up as" a person of color and could, therefore "understand the situation" of oppression in which the mentee found himself. Although the mentee argued with this reasoning by describing Whiteness in comparative terms, the mentor offered what he saw as additional evidence such as a "fake accent" and felt that the mentee did accept this denial of Whiteness. The mentor summarized his individual agency to offer the mentee understanding of racial oppression by telling the researcher, "He doesn't think of me as this White person. He thinks of me as someone who can relate to what he's going through ... I think he appreciates that, that I can understand him."

Not all stories of individual and race were representations of understanding. For example, the same mentor who thought he could connect with the mentee about racial oppression decided to hire a private tutor for a subject in which the mentee struggled. The mentor decided to hire a Black man who "fought his way through really difficult odds stacked against him." We found it interesting that this mentor perceived limits to the cross-race relationship and set up another kind of same-race relationship for the mentee. Still, the mentor's description of the decision was about the success of the set up rather than the nature of the relationship for the mentee. In this representation of success, there seemed to be reflected a traditional notion of morality that was based on the individual agency of the setup.

This valuation of actions based on the consequences for the mentor rather than the mentee was a common theme in the data. In one mentor's initial matching interview, for example, he said that he planned to enter into a mentoring relationship with a Latino mentee because "it look[ed] like something [the mentor] could feel good doing." Although this statement was preceded by the comment of, "Latinos have it hard," it was the positive feelings that he anticipated experiencing as a result of "giving back" that brought the mentor to the program.

The mentors' comments often reflected confusion when it came to race and their mentoring. One mentor expressed sadness and frustration with his mentee's unwillingness to speak with him about race, even after they attended a program-sponsored visit of an exhibit on race. When asked about race one mentor said, "We've talked about some of those kinds of issues .... We've had some of those conversations about issues like that. So they're not (pause) off-limits or anything," and offered an example of asking the mentee what the mentee thought about the characters in the bestselling novel at the time, *The Help*. In two different instances, the mentee in this relationship approached the mentor in order to expose a "racist teacher." The mentor reported having been at a loss for what to do in these two cases. The mentor's reaction of telling the mentee, "Well, do you want me to do something? Do you want me to go talk to somebody about it?" seemed to reflect a perspective based on individual agency. The mentor reported that the mentee reacted to this offer with, "Oh, no!" This reaction, along with the mentor's perspective based on individual agency, led us to believe that the mentor may have been struggling to understand the mentee when it came to race.

Another mentor also seemed to have a perspective of individual agency when it came to race, but in this case, felt as though she had agency. The mentor reported feeling that it was her role to "encourage [the mentee] to embrace her story." We found this mentor's perspective interesting in that not only did she claim this agency on her mentee's feeling about her own life story but also agency to tell what she knew of that story to the research team when asked to comment on the topic of race. Furthermore, this telling of the mentee's story was paired with an absence of storying any aspect of the White mentor's life. Still, the case was interesting to us because it was an example of action taken.

Another mentor described her role when it came to race as, "helping [the mentee's] mom to understand how life is for [the mentee]. Kind of what she is struggling with between American and Mexican culture." Yet another mentee argued, "Many of them don't even know what their own culture is," and that one of the purposes of the program and education, in general, was to bring White adults into the youth's lives who could help the youth "finally take pride in their culture." We found these three descriptions of agency similar in that the mentors perceived themselves to be taking an action of instruction about the experiences of the mentees.

These variations on agency and race, including actions taken based on perceptions of understanding, states of confusion, and valuation determined by consequences for the mentor rather than the mentee, all involved a perspective of individual agency when it came to race. These variations seemed to point towards an overall sense of the program as an individual intervention program for the very characteristic of being a youth of color. One mentor's summative comments on the purpose of the program illustrate this overall sense. She said, "I think [the program's] all very good. It's just that these kids are challenging. You know, they are challenges in their own way and that's why the program exists." Although this mentor did not explicitly name race in her comments, we interpreted them to reflect color-blindness (Bonilla-Silva, 2014) and used them in our argument about agency and race. Interpreted in this way, the positioning of the very being of color causing a youth to be a "challenge" for an individual mentor led us to ask questions about the hopes that the White mentors had for individual agency.

## 7    Success/Hopes for Agency

In an introductory letter to the mentee before even having met the mentee, one mentor wrote, "I would like to help you and your family in school. I worked at [a school] and helped many Latino/Hispanic families learn more about their children's school and communicate with their children's teachers. Also, I know that sometimes it is hard to be a Latino/Hispanic student living and going to school in the United States and I would like to support you." Another mentor stated in her initial placement interview that she was "interested in supporting Latino youth." We approached the interview data with a sense of the mentors as hopeful. We asked what emerged from these initial general senses of "supportive" hope.

One form of individual agency for which the mentors hoped was the installation of a meritocratic worldview. Merit was most often described as enacting "motivation" and "effort." The representations reflected valuing of these traits and what the mentors saw as the outcome indicators of the traits. In some cases, for example, mentors evaluated the mentees' families by the outcome indicators involved in the causal relationship they had in mind. One mentor described a mentee's mother by saying, "The good thing is his mom's really a good role model. She has worked hard. She just moved into a modest but nice home."

The mentors' narration of their own outcomes also indicated that they perceived outcomes as directly tied to merit. For example, one mentor said, "Hopefully just whatever influence that I have rubs off. You know. We live in a nice house .... That's what you get if you work hard when you're young and you go to a good school and put in effort." Another mentor attributed his family's multiple academic degrees to being "individually motivated" and "self-made." The meritocratic worldview reflected in such statements indicated a traditional notion of responsibility not only in the mentors' hopes for influencing the mentee but also in the content of the mentors' meritocratic worldviews.

The mentors hoped to directly instill a meritocratic worldview to the exclusion of attribution of structural factors such as racism. The mentor who explained that his own hard work directly led to ownership of his home said, "I'm hoping just the positive influence rubs off [on the mentee]." Another reported that in response to the mentee's question, "Why are you so rich?" the mentor not only situated his outcomes in his hard work towards good grades but also told the mentee that he could take an identical path to such outcomes. His lengthy description of this path indicated that he argued to the mentee that this path to being rich was independent of structural factors such as racism. For example, he said of the rich, "You know, they're not all White people. They're all different kinds of people." Another mentor reported telling a Black male mentee, "There's no reason why you can't .... The melanin in your skin ... like pigmentation, you know, it doesn't stop you from doing anything."

Another form of individual agency the mentors imagined was directly causing access to higher education. This form included actions such as walking through college campuses together, introducing mentees to college students and college alumni, increasing time away from home and family, and attempting to control outcomes important to the college application process. One mentor aimed to minimize the amount of time the mentee spent at home with the mentee's family under the reasoning that only time away from home would increase the likelihood of the mentee attending college. This mentor's individual efforts to find places or people that would take the mentee and independently pay for those places or people were continuous and driven by a sense of moral urgency. Another mentor said, "We are kind of getting her ducks lined up now. But it is very frustrating for me to get her scores lined up where they need to be .... Her scores aren't where they need to be." This case was interesting to us because the mentor represented herself as controlling an increase in her mentee's test scores in order to allow the mentee to attend college. This sense of control and causality reflects the objectivity and individualism involved in the traditional notion of moral responsibility.

Another causal relationship the mentors represented was between their interventions at the school and the attention paid to the mentees' academics. Several mentors described having met with teachers to demand greater expectations, resources, or consideration for the mentee. The mentors described outcomes of success as a result of these interventions. For example, one mentor argued that these interventions led to "better treatment" for the mentee. Interestingly, attention outcomes were the main focus of any schooling critique that appeared in the interviews. The causal relationship between interventions with teachers and attention outcomes for mentees reflected the objectivity and individualism involved in the traditional notion of moral responsibility. Furthermore, it seemed to us that the causal relationship also reflected this same notion when it came to the mentors' perceptions of teacher agency. In other words, they intervened in the individual agency of the mentees' teachers.

This dual layer of the traditional notion of moral responsibility was underlying the majority of the mentors' representations of success as mentors, but their representations of success were not about race. When about race, their representations of agency were stories of failure.

## 8 Agency and Race Failures

When about race, representations of agency were stories of mentors' failed individual agency. One mentor, for example, storied a long-standing attempt to change the behavior of two Latino mentees. We include his comments here in detail because they elicit such complex interpretation. "Basically what I have done with [the mentees] is for instance [they] look down when [they] talk to me ... I would say, 'Look. The deal with Anglos is: Look them in the eye and smile and if you can do that, you are going to get by in pretty good shape. If you look down then it shows them you don't think you are good as they are but if you look them in the eye then you are home free.'"

This mentor felt as though this attempt at agency had failed. Another part of this attempt was his demanding that the mentees thank him when the mentor did something for them as well as thanking "folks" when they did something for the mentees. Interestingly, this attempt, which we interpreted as disregarding power relations and therefore an exceptionally dangerous attempt at agency, was the only story the mentor told on the topic of race. The mentor named more than one topic that may have led to discussions on structures of racism but said that he avoided those topics with the mentee. He elaborated, "But we haven't sat down through the history of civil rights or discussing the ... the ... discrimination against immigrants either legal or illegal. Or documented or undocumented. That just hasn't been part of the equation."

In summary on the topic of race, the mentor said, "It's not a problem now. I'm sure they run into it but they don't run into it when they are with me so I don't know how big the effect is." We interpreted the mentor's feelings of agency failure and overall dismissal of race as likely related to one another.

In some cases the mentors who represented their individual agency to have failed attributed that failure to the mentees' families or racial groups. If failure was attributed to the family, the family's race was central to that assignment of causality. For example, one mentor attributed what she perceived as her failure to do "significant" activities with the mentee to what she described as the family's race-based practice of spending time with their child on the weekends and not allowing their child to stay overnight at the mentor's house. Of the program, this mentor said, "They threw me a curve when they gave me [the mentee] because of some cultural things I have to deal with and which are a big challenge."

Some mentors discussed their efforts at agency as everyday failures and named their only successes to be times in which they separated the mentee from the family. "Sending away" the mentees to camps and on vacations or trips, often in the company of White people, was common language that reflected the mentors' attribution of failure to the mentees' families or racial groups. Some mentors described their agency to be limited because they entered the mentees' lives too late. One mentor, for example, said that the mentor's influence of English provided the mentee with "focus and direction" that was not possible in the mentee's life before the mentor arrived. Although this representation was about language, the mentors' comments about language and race were often conflated so we interpreted it to be a representation supporting our interpretation that the mentors attributed their perceived agency failures to the mentees' families or racial groups.

## 9　Agency Failures Attributing Failure

Even though some described their mentoring to have no influence on the world, and sometimes attributed outcomes to structural factors, the White mentors' claims were still based on objectivity. For example, what Applebaum described as senses of control and choice were underlying their comments about what they perceived as either their own failure as mentors or their mentees' failures.

Therefore, although they sometimes attributed outcomes to structural factors, the mentors' representations of moralities were based on a traditional notion of moral responsibility that situated the mentors as autonomous and individualist agents. This position, as Applebaum argued, placed the mentors in a position of authority that was removed from that which was to be changed. Such a position, we argue, prevented a moral agency from emerging from a perspective of White complicity.

Sometimes the mentors attributed agency failures to individual characteristics of the mentees. The most common characteristic so described was what the mentors called "shyness" or "quietness." Many of the mentors were concerned that the mentees would be too quiet, shy, or not "open" or "outgoing" enough with the mentor, which would prevent the mentor from "being effective." This concern was so extreme that one mentor was worried that his future mentee would not be able to tell him the activities that the mentee enjoyed doing.

This wish for openness was linked to language of "trust." Interestingly, the mentors' representations indicated a perspective that the mentor relationship would be the only potential relationship of trust in the mentee's life. In other words, the mentors did not seem to recognize existing or potential relationships of trust within the mentees' families or communities. This exclusivity of the relationship seemed to us to be a source of power for the mentors. Representations of this desire for exclusive trust were marked by high level of emotional investment. Many mentors even repeatedly requested mentees who would fulfill this desire before the matches were even formed. Program staff described one match to have ultimately fallen apart due to the issue of openness.

Occasionally the mentors attributed agency failures to their own mentoring. One mentor, for example, explained the decline in the mentee's academic performance and lack of college scholarships to the mentor's failure of influence. Interestingly, however, the mentor's representation of this link situated the problem as being the mentor's own disappointment and bad feelings about being a mentor. In other words, the perceived harm in this situation was for the White mentor rather than the youth of color. Another mentor called himself a failure for not improving the mentee's grades, told the mentee, "You're making me look really bad."

## 10    Structural Factors

Some of the White mentors mentioned structural factors. We found it interesting that in each of these cases, the structural factors were in reference to the lives of the mentees or of youth of color in general, but never in reference to the mentors' own lives or the lives of Whites. For example, one mentor spoke of "institutional racism" being a "big topic" in her professional work and described herself as "in it together" with her Black colleagues and "kind of familiar with the Black community" but when asked about race and her relationship with her mentee said, "I don't know how to answer the question."

We were surprised to interpret that among the mentors who mentioned structural factors at play in the lives of their mentees or youth of color, none varied from representing a moral responsibility overwhelmingly based on individual agency. In other words, the few instances of this interpretation made our analysis more complex not only by presenting a multiplicity of views among the mentors but also by presenting a set of mentors with contradicting views. In some cases, mentors mentioned instances in their life stories when they were working in organizations that aimed to address structural factors of racism. For example, one mentor who worked for 12 years as part of a coalition for refugee rights mentioned several structural factors involved in the oppression of Latin@ immigrants. He said, "Latinos have it hard." He discussed economic oppression in historical context, imagined that youth at school often feel "like they don't belong," and he argued extensively for a Latin@-centered curriculum in schools. Despite these indicators of structural factors of influence, his representations still involved a sense of moral responsibility that was primarily based on individual agency, and in particular, individual agency through the mentoring relationship. For example, one of his main forms of individual agency in the relationship was to teach his mentee not to "quibble," or lie, which the mentor argued was a tendency of immigrants to do with their United States "hosts."

This contradiction of representation of moralities was something that emerged late in the analysis. We initially expected that each mentor would represent a moral responsibility of either the traditional individualistic nature or Applebaum's suggested subjective nature, but the seemingly contradictory nature of a structural explanation of racism but an objective and individualistic agency role in the mentoring relationship challenged our perceptions of the perspectives of White mentors in mentoring programs for youth of color. We argue that the contradicting views within the mentors' representations would be promising sites of possibility for a pedagogy of White complicity for mentoring.

## 11     Structural Factors and Race

When mentors did speak of structural factors involved in racism, this talk was limited to the experiences of immigrant and refugee groups. Although mentors usually did not use language that named racism, they sometimes used language such as "barriers," "school culture," or "intimidation" and we interpreted this language to point towards racism. In only one case did a mentor mention racism as it related to the experiences of a Black mentee, and in this case, the story reflected an understanding of racism as individual prejudice on the part of retail employees.

In one case a mentor named "barriers" that she imagined the mentee in the relationship to eventually face once the mentee attempted to acquire access to college and a job. The mentor's analysis of those barriers was limited to naming this general location and stating that "confronting" those barriers would be "pretty challenging" for the mentee. She cited the mentee's involvement in "extracurricular" activities, enrollment in honors and AP courses, and personal characteristics of "driven," "intelligent," and "outgoing" as "potential" against those barriers. We interpreted the mentor's analysis of the mentee's potential as she encountered access barriers to rely on an individual sense of agency. Still, we found it promising that this mentor was thinking in terms of structural barriers and also at least naming structural systems such as tracking and schooling activities outside of school.

General contextual or structural aspects that were mentioned across the data included languages spoken, vernaculars valued, customs during meal times, norms at school, family roles in home spaces, media representations of racial groups, and economic and job market fluctuations. Before their relationship even started one mentor hoped that she might "help [the mentee] negotiate the world." Another mentor named structural factors in his description of the purposes of the mentoring program. He said, "They're trying to reach kids that um, that should succeed but because of some, um, systemic or cultural factor that we don't quite understand, they don't succeed to their full ability." We found it interesting that this mentor named structural factors and their influence on outcomes for students but dismissed them with an all-encompassing claim of mystery. Although they were few and far between in the data, we interpreted the mentioning of structural topics as glimmers of possibility for a socially constructed subjectivity.

Another glimmer of possibility for a socially constructed subjectivity when it came to race shone in a cautionary approach to the mentoring. This mentor, who had extensive experience in formal service programs, seemed to implicitly question the Whiteness of individual agency. He explained that it was important to, "spend time, be patient, be an observer. It's not wise to jump in and try to change things. You have to respect parents as their own agents. Take time to get to know them and their context and perspective." The caution that this mentor mentioned reflected caution of the traditional notion of moral responsibility. Although the absence of reference to race paired with the context in which this statement was made likely indicates normalization of Whiteness, the mentor's sense of caution was an exception to the trend of representations of a traditional notion of moral responsibility.

We searched the data for cases in which the mentors attributed outcomes at least in part to structural factors. In these cases, the mentors spoke of social forces influencing outcomes in general but did not connect those forces to the outcomes of their mentees. For example, some mentors discussed connections between racial segregation and residential segregation, religion and race, racial tracking through differentiated exams, race and access to quality healthcare, and vernacular and race, but those discussions were never about the experiences of the mentees.

SOMEONE FABULOUS LIKE ME

Interestingly, those discussions were most often about the experiences of the mentors' White families over time rather than their current social contexts. Comments such as, "It's not a level playing field. Everyone doesn't start at the same place," were most often embedded as only an afterthought within meritocratic or eugenic comments about being "self-made" or "motivated." One mentor argued, for example, "You have to define your own potential." In one case a mentor spoke at length about the systematic injustice of racial tracking through differentiated test versions, arguing, "I think it's discriminating against them, to their own disadvantage, keeping them repressed, and they're not going to be able to achieve the same things as the other counter group, the White kids, if they're not being trained with the same level of intensity .... The people that are getting special treatment are the White kids .... It reinforces everything." This mentor argued for systematic change starting with intervention on the part of insider adults. However, although he firmly claimed, "I wouldn't want it for my kids. If I had kids, and they were getting a dumbed down test, because the school thought they weren't as bright, I'd be pissed. I would. You know? Why do you think my kid's not capable?" This outrage seemed to be limited to the hypothetical situation experienced by his own children should they have been children of color. He called on the interviewer to take action on this injustice, but for the mentor's own part, structural understanding of racism seemed to be paired with acceptance.

Tragically, the strongest manifestation of structural (mis)understanding was a perspective of "reverse racism." The most common view from this perspective was that in serving youth of color, the mentoring program was racist. The mentors who articulated this view spoke of the potential for the program to help White youth and suggested that the program be systematically altered to serve Whites. Mentors even used terms about race to forward arguments for this case. For example, two mentors said that such a policy would increase the "diversity" within the program on the grounds that a primary value of the program was diversity. Another mentor argued that her own White child should have been admitted as a mentee and claimed that the program created "reverse segregation." One mentor argued that a particular Black mentee be removed from the program and replaced with a White "brainiac kid" because the Black mentee did not seem to appreciate the mentor's agency enough, or, "did not want to receive" what the mentor had to "give." The mentor described the Black mentee's reception of programmatic benefits such as funding for test preparation courses as unjust and argued that the tall height, career success, and blue eye color of the mentor was wasted on "a short Black kid." A brief excerpt of the mentor's extensive comments on the subject follows. "My only observation about the program, the one thing that I do not like, I do not like that it is exclusively minorities. That I do not like. Because it sets kids aside that could benefit from the program. And, I think that is a flaw. I know, I understand the underlying premise of the program is institutional, built-in bias against minority groups, but I'll tell you what. It is biased against poverty. Struggling to get out of limitations imposed by one's circumstances is as real as any challenge a red kid or Black kid [faces]. And I feel very strongly about that."

This mentor reported that she raised this concern with the program director. Because the perspective was paired with an action, we interpreted this to be a strong indicator of the idea of "reverse racism." In addition, these comments suggest that the mentor could name the purposes of the program when it came to race yet still argued for "reverse racism." The excerpt echoes the well-documented misunderstanding of the role of a power differential in racism.

For an introductory text on this topic, we recommend Sensoy and DiAngelo's (2012), *Is everyone really equal?* This is an introduction to key concepts in social justice education. The mentors' argument for "reverse racism" extended beyond the program itself. Laughing when asked about societal discrimination against the mentee, one mentor named the mentee's parents of color as racist, arguing that the family was the only location of any racism. The mentor argued, "The racism goes that way," and described herself as suffering from this idea of "reverse racism" due to her Whiteness.

## 12 Pedagogy for Mentoring (Possibilities for White Complicity Pedagogy)

We agree with Applebaum's claim that for those practicing social justice pedagogy, White denial of complicity is a chronic problem. She argued for a White complicity pedagogy, which is grounded in her rearticulated notion of moral responsibility. For Applebaum (2010), White complicity work is necessary for anti-racist relationships between Whites and people of color: "[F]or White people to join in alliances with the victims of racism to challenge systemic racial oppression White people have to acknowledge their complicity. This means being vigilant about White moral agency because such moral agency can ironically obstruct a genuine engagement with those who experience racial oppression" (p. 6). Our analysis suggests that for the twelve White mentors in this study, a subjectivity of White complicity was not available for moral agency in the mentoring. In this discussion section, we consider points in the data that seem to us to be possibilities for moving towards a subjectivity of White complicity.

Applebaum (2007) has called for a re-articulation of the notion of moral responsibility in education, moving from the centering of Whites' emotions

SOMEONE FABULOUS LIKE ME

to instead complicity, a move that may allow for moral agency that is based in relationships. Instead of a White privilege pedagogy, then, this would be a White complicity pedagogy (Applebaum, 2010). Viewed this way, mentoring could become another education space in which Whites and youth of color are brought into a relationship. Applebaum (2010) acknowledged, "… I have not offered any lesson plans or concrete pedagogical suggestions. There is, however, no formula for how to do White complicity pedagogy" (p. 197). She encouraged researchers to share their attempts at and ideas for White complicity pedagogy, and here we deploy Whiteness studies in order to identify possible entry points for a White complicity pedagogy for mentoring. These entry points include (a) the Whiteness of "exposure," (b) stereotypes of families of color, (c) historical programming, and, (d) family narratives.

## 13      Whiteness of "Exposure"

Mentors often reported ways in which they would try to "better" the mentees in ways to expose them to what they viewed as cultural activities. These activities included activities such as live performances, institutional displays of art or history, and international travel. In addition, mentors made valuing statements about their mentees, themselves, and their own children based on exposure to those same activities. Underlying the representations of exposure was an overwhelming sense of Whiteness, which Applebaum (2010) described as Whites' acting with the sense that Whites see themselves as morally good. In the mentors' representations, we interpreted not only a sense of moral goodness but also moral superiority. The representations involved perceptions of agency moving this exposure as a mechanism for the White mentors to better the students of color. We argue that the choices made to expose students to culture often are void of efforts to value students' of color cultures but are rather a way to expose them to Whites' ideas of culture that is best for bettering students' outcomes. One mentor even expressed that the very act of bringing his White family members into contact with Latino youth was a successful solution to the problem he perceived the "fairly closed" "Latino community" to have of being "not exposed to what's out there."

Even before the mentors were assigned mentees, the mentors often spoke of their aims to better the mentees by exposing them to what they viewed as cultural activities. Some expressed "want" for a mentee who would be, for example, "open to having their life open" or "flexible … wants to better himself." In addition, mentors sometimes attributed the success of themselves and their own children to a sense of "interest" acquired as a result of a more general sort of exposure to "the wider world." These stories of success and hope, as well as the dominance of the theme of exposure, led us to question how the Whiteness of exposure related to the sense of individual agency.

Several themes related to exposure suggested that the White mentors believed they morally must bring their agency for the purpose of bettering the mentees through exposure to what they viewed as cultural activities. This sense of moral urgency was Whitely. By Whitely, we mean that this sense of moral urgency invoked an ideology of White supremacy. One theme indicated that mentors perceived White culture and African American culture to be dichotomous, defined as good and bad forms of culture respectively. For example, one mentor made the mentee watch Shakespeare "and stuff like that" as a substitute for "Tyler Perry movies." Another theme displayed was the notion that mentoring is best achieved through this cultural exposure that is attributed to White culture. Another major theme we noticed was that mentors viewed this cultural exposure to be an important condition of their participation as mentors. For example, mentors revealed in their initial interviews the "types" of students they were willing to work with and their plans for exposure activities as the basis of their mentoring relationship. Lastly, another theme was understanding mentees of color and mentees' families of color through negative stereotypes. The holding of these stereotypes seemed to compel the White mentors to expose students to what they viewed as good examples of White culture.

These themes usually overlapped in the mentors' representations and this overlapping indicated the deep-seatedness of the Whiteness of "exposure." For example, one mentor's description of her initial interview to become a mentor exemplified justification of this particular representation of morality in its extension to her views of the perceptions of others involved in the mentoring relationship. She projected, "You know, I said I loved shows and I'd love to expose [the mentee] to some cultural things that I like. Anyway, I remember the one thing that really .... Everything sounded fine to them but the one thing her mom actually said was she wanted to expose her to my world." We found this comment to be an especially complex indicator of Whiteness because of the Whiteness underlying the mentor's claim that the student's mother subscribed to Whiteness, attributing the mentor's own meaning to the mother's term of the mentor's "world." This attribution of meaning attests to the power of Whiteness.

## 14 Stereotypes of Families of Color

The White mentors' representations of Whiteness were intimately tied to stereotypes of families of color. The mentor's comments that illustrated Whiteness

SOMEONE FABULOUS LIKE ME

continued on to indicate dormant stereotypes of families of color. As the mentor continued to describe the mother's wishes to have the student exposed to "her world" she further explained, "She's an assistant schoolteacher so she's not an unsophisticated person at all. But, you know, I think she meant whatever I like to do is fine and that I didn't have to, you know, be directing her towards, you know, healthy African American type activities." We believe that in order to support Applebaum's suggestion for a White complicity pedagogy (Applebaum, 2010), mentors work to understand the ways in which it is important to challenge stereotypes involved in a mindset of complicity. In this case of the mentor feeling that it is her job to expose the mentee to her world and not "healthy African American type activities," we would ask, What are "unhealthy African American activities"? What are the stereotypes that lie dormant within mentors' minds?

When it comes to stereotypes, mentors described families in deficit ways. This view often manifested in comparisons between the mentor's family and the mentee's family. One way in which the mentors narrated this comparison was through a general description of and hierarchical valuing of "life" or "living." For example, one mentor described her forty years in the community as "a good life," enjoying success at competition with her peers in school, success at acquiring educational degrees, and success at becoming a wife and mother. She compared this "good life" with the very different life of her mentee and said she wanted her mentee to see what a good life was by seeing "how we live." She even expressed confidence in knowing what life was like at the mentee's high school. Before she ever met her mentee, another mentor said in her initial interview that she would, "help her learn how to negotiate the world." This comment indicated a perception that the mentee, perhaps because the mentee was a youth of color, was not already negotiating the world and had a deficit of resources from which to learn to do so.

In addition to this deficit narrative about "life" in general, the White mentors specified aspects of family in their deficit framing. For instance, mentors were concerned that youth of color did not have any "role models" in their lives. One mentor argued that kids of color "just need a dream and a hope in the future" and hoped to teach kids of color that their "potential" was not limited to their families. One mentor had trouble articulating anything that the mentee might have learned from his family other than a sense that "education is not important" and a pattern of being "well groomed." More than one mentor argued that the families of color did not "value" or "emphasize" education. Mentors spoke of characteristics such as incarceration, underemployment, addiction, relationship dynamism, and cohabitation as typical of families of color.

Stereotypes of families of color seemed to drive this deficit narration of families and life in general. Mentors often nested these stereotypes in attempts to engage with the researchers in what Christine Sleeter (1994) called "White racial bonding." More specifically, the mentors used phrases such as "you know" to bracket comments about families of color in attempts at "affirming a common stance on race related issues, legitimatizing particular interpretations of groups of color, and drawing conspiratorial we-they boundaries" (Sleeter, 1994, p. 34). Finally, we found it tragic that most of the White mentors were surprised and at a loss for words when the researchers asked them what the mentees learned from their families. The attempts at White racial bonding and the loss for words regarding learning from family may be two promising entry points into White complicity pedagogy and the topic of stereotypes of families of color.

One specific stereotype within the mentors' representations was a stereotype of an angry mentee. One mentor planned to charge a school official with teaching the mentee how to, "deal with anger, or not necessarily anger, but what it is to be a Black man." This comment assigned the characteristic of angry to the nature of being a Black male, and in framing being angry as a problem also framed being a Black man as a problem to be solved. Another description that pointed to the angry mentee stereotype for youth of color was the term "negative," as in a negative kid or a kid with a negative attitude. From an instance in which a Black mentee retaliated against a White aggressor's physical push, one mentor directly generalized, "You know, African Americans are the, have to show that they're tougher and stronger .... It's like he wants to be that tough, he can't let his race down or something like that .... What it means to be an African American male, you know." This mentor brought his analysis to action by encouraging the mentee and other Black males to tolerate microaggressions (Smith, Hung, & Franklin, 2011).

Another stereotype within the mentors' representations was what we would call a "but" stereotype. This included all positive evaluative characteristic statements about mentees that were either explicitly or implicitly in comparison to negatively evaluative characteristics (Hall, 1997). For example, mentees were youth of color "but": "nice," "very nice," "good," "sweet-natured," "capable" .... Sometimes these labels seemed to be strung together in an effort to convince the interviewer of the mentee's merits. One mentor, for example, when asked how her experience had compared to her expectations for the mentoring program, responded that the mentee was "such a super kid, she's a great kid, she really is, she is a good person. And she works hard." In this case, the mentoring experience as a whole seemed to be centered on this "but" stereotype. If the mentors had been describing White youth, we argue that the characteristics within this "but" stereotype may not have been mentioned but instead assumed.

## 15   Historical Programming

We were surprised not to hear more of the mentors discussing the complicated nature of historical context of race in the city in which the mentoring program was being offered. Although a thorough analysis of this point is beyond the scope of this paper, the research team noticed that several parents, when asked about race, responded with the historical context and the impact on their lives. Mentors, on the other hand, rarely spoke of historical context. In one case a mentor discussed her experience of speaking with a close friend, an African American woman, who grew up in the area. The area she recalls had dividing lines of which she learned through her friend's experience. She said, "My friends … also grew up here … and their parents would tell them, 'Don't cross the line into Carverville.' I'm kind of aware of some history of this area where they grew up." The history the mentor mentions is prevalent today, and we argue that historical programming would be a promising entry point for White complicity pedagogy for mentoring.

According to the U.S. Department of Commerce Census Bureau (2011), Carverville's 2011 population was estimated at 58,011 people, 72.8% of whom were White, 9.7% Black, 0.3% American Indian, and 11.9% Asian. This compared to the state's population of 68% White, 21.5% Black, 1.3% American Indian, and 2.2% Asian. Also, it's important to note that in Carverville at the time of the study 48.3% of people owned their home, and the median value of those homes was $356,400 as compared to $149,100 for the state. The median household income for the city was $52,785 as compared to $45,570 for the state. In Carverville 22.2% of people were living below the poverty level as compared to 15.5% for the state. The per capita money income in Carverville was $33,710 compared to $24,745 in the state. The state population was 9,656,401, and in Carverville the population represented .5% of the state's nearly 10 million residents, which means that people in Carverville during the time of the study made an average of $10,000 more than people in the state.

The mentorship program was created as "a district-wide student support program designed to improve the achievement of African-American and Latino students by promoting success in multiple developmental realms." Because the program considered race to be central to the population it served, we feel that it's important to acknowledge that while race was important in the implementation in the program, the White mentors lacked the understanding of how the complicated nature of race and racism are threaded through the current status of the program.

## 16 Family Narratives: "It All Worked Out"

When describing their life stories to the research team, many of the White mentors represented themselves as having been marginalized in some way during their childhood but then later in life experiencing things to have become "all worked out." Their representations of things having worked out for them were heavily situated within family narratives. Whites' family narratives may be an entry point for White complicity pedagogy for mentoring. One narrative strategy that Whiteness scholars have connected to the deflection of complicity is Whites' comparison of their White selves to their White racist families (Applebaum, 2010). In this study Whites storied race out of their family narratives.

Although all of the mentors experienced White privilege and, based on the representations of their occupations and life stories, class privilege, the mentors did not speak of sources of privilege. Instead, the mentors represented a type of inevitability or naturalness to their privilege having somehow "worked out" or they attributed their privilege to two sources: their individual actions or what they called a "positive family," "solid values." The mentors' inattention to their privilege was exemplified in the comments of a mentor who viewed her current economic outcomes as having "all worked out." Interestingly, one mentor mentioned her privilege, saying, "I think keeping perspective of my privilege and of my place in this world is pretty important." However, the mentor did not elaborate on this perspective she claimed to keep. Although it was not clear in the study what work the mentor had done on investigating her own privilege, the mention of the privilege was the only exception we found to the representation of privilege's naturalness.

In addition to a naturalness to privilege somehow having "worked out," the mentors also described a naturalness to their abilities for gaining privilege. For example, one mentor described technical understanding in his field of work as, "It came easily to me." Sometimes this sense of naturalness was tied to a description of themselves as "self-motivated" as well as to a description of contexts in which ultimate privileges are gained being "tough" territory that required such motivation and naturalness of ability. Markers of this "tough" territory included problems of the privileged, such as student loan debt, sustenance of profit flow, and the expansion of the hiring of employees. One mentor argued that in his field of work, "We just have to fight for our life."

## 17 Influence of Mentoring Programming

Although we did not study the influences of mentoring programming on the mentors' representations of moralities, we do claim that mentor programming may have possibilities for influencing mentoring relationships. By mentor programming, we mean formal mentor programming designed for prospective and current mentors.

One interpretation that led us to claim that mentor programming may have a possibility for influence was that mentors' comments about mentor programming included perspectives on race that seemed similar to the mentors' perspectives on race. For example, when mentors spoke of the program's purposes for matching White mentors with youth of color they claimed a sense of Whiteness on the part of the mentoring program. A typical mentor representation of programming's Whiteness was that the purpose of the program was to have Whites work with youth of color in order to, "you know, kind of show them the other side of the tracks, try to expand their horizons." Another mentor explained that her programming gave her the message that the purpose of the program was to "broaden" the experiences of the mentees. Although we did not study the nature of the mentor programming, the mentor interviews suggested that the mentors were at least hearing messages of Whiteness through mentor programming about race. The activity report forms that the mentors were to fill out even asked the mentors if they "took a student to a cultural activity outside of their normal experience." Messages of Whiteness seemed to be underlying the program as a whole.

In addition to messages of Whiteness, mentor programming seemed to offer White mentors insufficient discourses with which to think and speak about race. We found it interesting that many of the mentors seemed to want to speak of mentor programming about race but were unsure about how to express their views. For example, one mentor stumbled to describe his mentoring programming, saying, "I'm not sure what the right phrasing is. But they … um, a very classical, social, um, counseling philosophy. You know. They bring up the disadvantaged and the disadvantaged here are people of color. So it's very …." This particular mentor spoke of race somewhat more than the other White mentors, and we argue that his struggle to find and use discourses about race and his mentor programming may be a location of possibility for White complicity pedagogy for mentoring.

Data related to the mentors also suggested that program staff sought mentor pedagogy about race. For example, an initial interviewer felt "concerned" about one prospective mentor, who the interviewer felt had, "some assumptions/expectations about working with students of color and students from poor families …. We need to pick a good student and monitor her match to make sure she doesn't stumble." Staff comments from initial interviews indicated not only a desire but also an urgent need for pedagogy on race. In the above comment, a White complicity pedagogy might offer staff a way to ask about matching policy for mentors with problematic assumptions about race, about valuing language such as "good student," and about the staff's own assumptions reflected in evaluative comments such as, "I would recommend matching her with a fairly stable and confident child from a supportive family."

## 18      Cautions and Further Directions

We recognize the underlying Whiteness of our move to suggest possibilities for a White complicity pedagogy for mentoring. This claim to know reflects a "White arrogant certainty about one's ability to know" (Applebaum, 2010, p. 184). Cris Mayo (2010) has called for a centering of not knowing instead of knowing, but even with this in mind, we have still arrived in this work to claims of knowing. We agree with Mayo, as well as with Applebaum (2010) in her claims that storying involves never having "arrived" (p. 186), yet as the field of mentoring studies involves audiences poised for programmatic actions and the research team seeks to bring considerations of Whiteness to those discussions, we decided on representation for explicit possibility rather than on storying. Through this representation is certainly a way that Whiteness finds yet another way to hide. A direction of our future work on Whiteness and mentoring is a storying representation for the audience of aspiring and practicing White mentors.

We also recognize that an analysis of the representations of White mentors attends to the harm done through the structuring of mentoring relationships rather than on the experiences of the harmed. Attention to the harm rather than the experiences of the harmed is a manifestation of Whiteness (Applebaum, 2010). Therefore, we emphasize that the analysis of White mentors' representations is important only as a supplemental contribution to the wider work of the research team.

Representations of the mentors are representations performed to a particular audience: an evaluation research team—a Whitened entity from a White-dominated place, speaking of the mentors in White discourse communities, in cohort with the White program leader. Still, all representations are performances; there is never an essential story.

In this chapter, we claim multiple possibilities for a White complicity pedagogy. From the field of social justice education as well as from our own experiences as educators and learners we know that engaging Whites with their own complicity is a complex and uncertain project. Applebaum's (2010) work helps us to understand Whites' responses to White complicity pedagogy in terms of Whiteness instead of in terms of individual reactions: "[I]t is not

SOMEONE FABULOUS LIKE ME

easy to get White people to consider their complicity. Denials of complicity are not understood to be 'denials' but because of White ignorance masquerade as White common sense" (p. 41). This understanding of Whites' responses sustains our work with Whites and often sustains Whites' own work on their White complicity. More specifically, in our experiences, Whites in the process of coming to understand their own responses to ideas of White complicity in terms of Whiteness have sprung from locations of resistance and paralysis. We do not see the possibilities offered here as solutions for racism. Rather, they may be additional entry points for those involved in pedagogical work aiming for anti-racist relationships.

White complicity pedagogy is distinct from White privilege pedagogy, which dominates social justice education. While Whites can engage with White privilege pedagogy all the while remaining personally removed from responsibility for racism, White complicity pedagogy intimately links Whites with racism. Applebaum (2010) explained this distinction of assumption between the two pedagogies: "[W]hite complicity pedagogy begins with the principle that the recognition of complicity, not just privilege, is the starting point for White engagement with systemic racial injustice" (p. 180). We find this distinction to be especially important for cross-race mentoring, as our interpretations indicate that the systemic bringing together of Whites and youth of color into a relationship in this mentoring program was a reinscribing of racism. Given this practice's evaluation by the mentoring field as state-of-the-art and the entrenchment of the institution of mentoring as it is currently programmed, the consequences evoke a sense of pedagogical urgency.

Applebaum (2010) envisioned White complicity pedagogy to involve uncertainty, which is a concept that mentoring as it is currently structured rejects. Mentoring brings White mentors into mentoring relationships under the premise that the mentor can, should, and will do something about a problem through the mentoring relationship. This premise is based on an individual and autonomous concept of responsibility. Applebaum (2010) argued, "Because [traditional] notions of responsibility center the question 'what can I do?' rather than the question 'what needs to be done?' they can encourage moral solipsism, heroism, and White narcissism ... I call for a ... rearticulated notion of moral responsibility [that] does not focus on guilt but instead emphasizes uncertainty, vulnerability and vigilance" (p. 5). These twelve White mentors' representations of moralities indicate a centering of the question "what can I do?" for mentors rather than the question "what needs to be done?" for anti-racism. Perhaps, then, an emphasis on uncertainty, vulnerability, and vigilance through a White complicity pedagogy for mentoring might not only challenge the moral solipsism, heroism, and White narcissism and the consequences enacted through mentoring relationships between Whites and youth of color but also allow for movement towards understanding of what needs to be done for anti-racist relationships.

Even if the direction of White complicity from Whiteness studies were to be promising for mentoring, we are left with critical questions about cross-race mentoring involving White mentors. What might a White complicity pedagogy look like for mentoring? How would White mentors engaged in a White complicity pedagogy represent their relationships, and how might those relationships be different from the relationships for which mentoring currently sets the stage? We argue that a White complicity approach to mentoring would necessarily involve not only the notion of individual White complicity but also institutional White complicity. Furthermore, acknowledgment of White complicity involved in cross-race mentoring involving White mentors and youth of color characterized as in need of these particular types of relationships with the White mentors might cease cross-race mentoring programs involving White mentors. Finally, we recognize that a movement towards what needs to be done might involve an implosion of the institution of mentoring as it is currently programmed in favor of the structuring of relationships more anti-racist. We anticipate soon learning of possibilities for mentoring upon this perhaps welcome implosion of cross-race mentoring as it is currently constructed.

### References

Applebaum, B. (2007). White complicity and social justice education: Can one be culpable without being liable? *Educational Theory, 57*(4), 453–467.

Applebaum, B. (2010). *Being White, being good: White complicity, White moral responsibility, and social justice pedagogy.* Lanham, MD: Lexington Books.

Bonilla-Silva, E. (2014). *Racism without racists : Color-blind racism and the persistence of racial inequality in America* (4th ed.) Lanham, MD: Rowman & Littlefield Publishers, Inc.

Hall, S. (1997). *Representation: Cultural representations and signifying practices.* London & Thousand Oaks, CA: Sage Publications.

Mayo, C. (2010). Anti-racist White philosophical address. In G. Yancy (Ed.), *The center must not hold: White women philosophers on the Whiteness of philosophy* (pp. 211–226). Lanham, MD: Roman & Littlefield.

Sensoy, O., & DiAngelo, R. (2012). *Is everyone really equal: An introduction to key concepts in social justice education.* New York, NY: Teachers College Press.

Sleeter, C. (1994). A multicultural educator views White racism. *The Education Digest, 59*(9), 33–36.

Smith, W. A., Hung, M., & Franklin, J. D. (2011). Racial battle fatigue and the miseducation of Black men: Racial microaggressions, societal problems, and environmental stress. *Journal of Negro Education, 80*(1), 63–82.

U.S. Census Bureau. (2011). *Quick facts.* Retrieved from https://www.census.gov/en.html

Yancy, G. (Ed.). (2010). *The center must not hold: White women philosophers on the Whiteness of philosophy.* Lanham, MD: Roman & Littlefield.

CHAPTER 3

# Class Crossings: Mentoring, Stratification and Mobility

*George Noblit, Danielle Parker Moore and Amy Senta*

## 1 Introduction

> *... I picked up Luis (a pseudonym) in the end of the fourth grade. He is now a freshman at [local high school]. We have had a good relationship. Luis ... was somewhat shy in the beginning. He has got an older brother who is a sophomore now in high school and then a younger brother who is also my mentee. So I have two mentees. At any rate [mentee] has come out a fair amount in the last year or show. I think around everyone he is more outgoing. He is a good kid and not crazy about academics, prefers soccer to academics and but we have had a good relationship. I spent a fair amount of time one summer tutoring him in math though I don't see that as a mentor's mission .... Ummm ... the job or whatever. But when he was interested he was a quick study. And I could tell pretty quick if we were going to have a good session or it was going to go somewhat slow because his mind was somewhere else. And he is doing maybe average work in high school and it varies it never is outstanding. His brother, his older brother is an excellent student. His younger brother has got some problems which I will get into shortly. But he is a good kid and the family is very supportive. They have ... the mother has been to a number of parent teacher conferences and she never misses anything she is supposed to go to. The younger brother, [mentee] has a younger brother who is in the 4th grade and his name is [younger mentee], so this past summer told [mentee] that I was going to be his mentor. That they would let me work with [mentee] also, which is a little switch up on the way the system works. Anyway, I asked [staff], I told him I would be happy to take on [younger mentee] because a lot of times, [younger mentee] would go with us anyway when we were doing something. And so [younger mentee] has got me. He is a bit behind in school though I think he is a hard worker and he really likes to please. So I think he will get caught up.*

A good mentor knows a lot about his or her mentee. A good mentor develops a close relationship with the family and is supportive of the parents. A good

CLASS CROSSINGS 63

mentor does what is needed even if it a bit outside the usual role of the mentor. We see much of this in the quote above from Brian Dieter (a pseudonym). Brian got on well with the older son and with the parents and so it seemed as if it would be okay for him to take on the second son. The mentoring program saw him as doing a 'good enough' job that adding the second son seemed reasonable. If the story ended here, we could reasonably say there is something to learn from this mentoring relationship. It would suggest possibly some promising practices or ways of understanding mentoring that may be helpful to other mentors.

Yet the story does not end here. The mentoring relationship with the older son came apart. Of course, many mentoring relationships come apart and in many different ways. Relationships are fragile affairs and cross-race, cross-class relationships such as this one are not always easy to develop or sustain. Further, it is not always bad for relationships to come apart. Indeed, Gold Medal asks for a 2 year commitment from the mentors—not a lifetime. Mentors move, have life changes and competing commitments. We heard all of these, and more, in the interviews we conducted with mentors. Mentees similarly move and move on. Brian himself had an earlier mentee whose family moved back to Mexico six months after Brian began to serve as the mentor. Mentees also experience life changes that make mentoring less a priority and dating, peer groups, new family members, etc. all can undercut a mentoring relationship. All this is reasonable and seemingly natural even if it makes sustaining a mentoring relationship difficult.

The purpose of this book, however, is to take a critical look at mentoring as a social phenomenon based in our extensive study of one program, Gold Medal (a pseudonym). We are taking on a critical perspective precisely because we have concluded from our reading of the literature that while mentoring is a valued human relationship it is often treated as an unbridled 'good' thing. Our studies, though, found mentoring to be more complex than this and involving wide ranging social issues that are only occasionally discussed in the literature, particularly issues surrounding differences in social status and regard. Nevertheless, Gold Medal, our evaluation found, was a highly effective program and thus, while we encourage the reader to remember the unique aspects of Gold Medal in making any generalizations, this means that our critiques should not be dismissed as the result of a poorly executed program. Indeed, Brian saw Gold Medal as effective and lauded their preparation of him as a mentor:

> I think ... a really good training program ... they had several meetings with prospective mentors that [staff] had previously interviewed and then they had one of the meetings—meetings were almost like dramas, little workshops bringing up various incendiary questions or situations. And then we had some existing mentors came and talked and I think

maybe one or two brought mentees and I think on the last day we maybe they were a number of mentors that came. I am not sure. But at any rate, it was a very good training program.

Gold Medal in many ways is all about race. It serves students of color and explicitly works on racial identity. Gold Medal is tightly linked to the school district's efforts to improve racial equity in schooling outcomes. The mentoring relationship is usually cross-race, given the demographics of the locality. It also works with parents of color to help them advocate for their children. Race is implicated in almost all that it does. However, race never stands alone if one is to believe critical race theory (Crenshaw, 1995). Instead, race is "intersectional" with gender, sexuality, and social class. One experiences all of these together, if variably, in one's life experiences.

As we all know, race and class are interpolated. In other chapters in this book, the authors have addressed race in some detail. They do not ignore class but treat it as part of race and of the mentoring relationship. In this chapter, we wish to switch the lens to first consider social class and then race. This is not a point of disagreement with the other authors but rather a switch in perspective that hopefully reveals dynamics not otherwise as evident. We do not claim social class is the dominant factor affecting mentoring nor do we claim to be omniscient. We do not 'know' if social class is the key part of the story of the 'coming apart' of the mentoring relationship Brian had with his mentee. However, we will assert that analytically social class seems to make sense of part of it and when 'crossed' with race has much to say about mentoring relationships. Thinking in terms of class then, we argue, is valuable in both research and practice concerning mentoring.

## 2 Social Class as a Variable

Social class is not a major theme in mentoring research for many reasons. First, mentoring research usually uses a psychological and/or social psychological perspective. Social class in such a perspective is but an explanatory variable. Variability in income or education can explain part of other relationships of interest but class is also a lived experience that is deeply grounded in history and in relations among those of different classes, as well as other forms of difference. Class dynamics are not the focus of mentoring studies. Class is thus reduced to a variable. Second, mentoring, in general, and of youth in particular assumes that difference is necessary for mentoring to be effective. The mentor is to bring their extended life experience to the novice. In youth mentoring, we often want mentors who can aid the youth in becoming more than they or their family currently is. Here social class is at play but euphemized. This reliance on euphemism is no doubt part of the American myths of being a classless society. Witness how quickly in political discourse discussion 'class warfare' is claimed when class differences are discussed. Third, and relatedly, the adult life experience desired in mentors is also normative—there is something valued in the adult that is lacking in the mentee. Here the message is that one should want to take on the statuses the adult represents because they are better than the statuses of the mentee and mentee's family. This is a classic deficit model portrayal. Fourth, the portrayals of class in American society also assumes that statuses are matters of choice. It assumes that youth control their destinies and that there are not significant forces that militate against such choices.

Thus it not surprising that mentoring research and mentoring programs do not address social class differences directly. The persistence of social class (as well as race) difference is not spoken about directly because it is an implicit curriculum of mentoring: class is a variable not a social formation; the middle class has something to teach the working class; the middle class is better than the working class; and finally you can choose to change your class position. We will return to these points in way of conclusion but for now, they serve to set the stage to better understand how Brian 'did' social class and how that way of 'doing class' contributed to the demise of the mentoring relationship.

## 3    Brian and Race

In cross-race mentoring relationships there are many pitfalls. Racial differences in experience, language and interpretation can make common ground hard to recognize, let alone achieve. However, there is reason to believe that whites can work across race sufficiently to help youth of color. Indeed, this is premise of research on culturally relevant practice (Castagno & Brayboy, 2008). In this research, there are some themes that seem to explain how whites can effectively work across race (cf. Ladson-Billings, 1995). While there is some variability in relative emphasis placed on these themes, it does seem clear that: (1) whites need to be experienced in relations with people of color; (2) whites need to work as allies with parents and the communities of color; (3) whites should develop caring relationships with youth of color; (4) whites should explicitly teach the 'culture of power' (Delpit, 1988) that is hidden for youth of color; (5) whites should assume that the youth and their parents are capable (Moll, Soto-Santiago, & Schwartz, 2013); and (6) whites should directly work to enhance these capabilities.

This list is of course all too simplistic and reductionistic. However, it is sufficient to serve our argument that when it comes to race Brian seems to have many of the characteristics researchers see as important. Brian has worked with immigrant groups for years, had extensive international experience, and through marriage and life was sensitized to issues of language and race. We want to be clear that we are not arguing Brian is an anti-racist or full-blown white ally to people of color. Yet Brian may be 'the best we can expect' in a white mentor in regards to race. Thus, we will argue, it is his social class and how it is crossed up with race that must be addressed to explain the failure of the mentoring relationship. Brian, for us, is but one case of how mentors 'do class' with their mentees.

In this chapter we will examine how the mentors talked about their relationship with their mentees and analyze how this was 'doing class.' The data for this chapter were drawn from the mentor interviews (n = 17). For our coding and analysis we used Bourdieu's concepts of economic, social and cultural capital. These will be discussed below. To analytically focus on social class we excluded data that spoke to race. This, as we have acknowledged, is simply an analytic decision, race and class are intersectional. However, for the purposes of this book we think it useful to 'see' class. Our analysis can then be compared to the chapters more focused on race and to better discern what each brings to our understanding and critique of mentoring.

## 4 Social Class in Mentoring Research

Mentoring research has an interesting history. One the one hand, it is tightly tied to practice. Many of the studies are more or less evaluations of particular programs and, when not evaluations, the data sets are largely derived from programs. The logic has been to demonstrate that mentoring (and/or specific mentoring programs) works (or not), for whom and under what conditions. Our read is that to date this research program has been largely successful in justifying that mentoring is valuable and that certain practices seem promising. However, I would also argue that the result is that mentoring research as a field is notably circumscribed. In the second edition of the *Handbook of Youth Mentoring* (Dubois & Karcher, 2014), there are links being drawn to wider contexts (youth development, for example) and to applied fields of knowledge (prevention science, for example). Cultural perspectives are also explored. For us, these are all positive signs of mentoring research coming of age as a field of study in its own right. Yet, we would argue that for mentoring research to fully develop, it will need to reconsider its relation to social (and

CLASS CROSSINGS

other) theory, and develop conceptualizations that do more than characterize practice, as important as that is. In some sense, this book is such an attempt. It says in part that we learned about effective practice (and program) and now have larger questions about the meaning of the phenomenon. Our take here is heavily theoretical. Drawing on a set of critical theories, we ask of effective practice—how is it embedded in wider social phenomenon? The *Handbook* (Dubois & Karcher, 2014) begins this move, and beginnings beget a journey of exploration and change.

Deutsch, Lawrence, and Henneberger (2014) in their *Handbook* chapter on social class document how social class has been addressed in existing mentoring research and present a theoretical conceptualization of social class. This represents a significant step towards developing mentoring research as a field of *study*. Notably they conclude: "Although, there is little empirical research as to whether or how social class influences mentoring, a growing body of work suggests it might" (Deutsch, Lawrence, & Henneberger, 2014, p. 185). They also note that there are important definitional issues with social class, and offer a distinction between "material" (financial resources) and "cultural" (values, beliefs and norms) definitions of social class and also connect the latter to the potential for a collective, class identity. They reveal that in existing studies social class is conceived and measured as an attribute of the person and/ or family. In mentoring research, then, social class elides into socio-economic status. The authors offer a model that pushes beyond the limited conception of social class in the research and in doing so distinguish between class background and "moderating factors" (p. 179) such as material and environmental resources and social capital. This distinction points to an image of social class as less an attribute of a person and more polycentered—in and outside of the person per say. Resources and social capital are conceptualized as being more external.

This is a significant move and changes the view used in current mentoring research. However, we argue that this move signals much more than this. It signals a concept of social class that is embedded in social institutions and social practices. A view, that if we take it even further, offers the potential to consider mentoring as constitutive of social class. In this view, mentoring is 'classing,' as much as helping, youth. Mentoring may hold out the hope of class mobility but this should also be regarded as a form of 'doing class' on, and with, youth.

This view of class may be rather different from that in existing research on mentoring, but it is one that has a long history in sociology. After all, Marx (1867) saw capitalism as creating class formations that stratified society and created social conditions that people then inhabited. In this, ideologies such as meritocracy mask a set of social practices of division:

... dominant groups develop standards based on their own characteristics and customs and expect others to emulate them .... They also create myths about human features related to race, ethnicity, class and gender that mark, label, brand and stigmatize others as outsiders .... Their power is maximized when the *us* and *them* is seen as fundamental and irreversible. (Brantlinger, 2003, pp. 3–4)

Probably the leading recent social theorist of social class is the late Pierre Bourdieu. He drew the distinction between cultural, social, symbolic and economic capitals that has been picked up in many studies of social class. Each of these had distinctive meanings for Bourdieu, and are more complex than many acknowledge in their empirical work. For example, his discussion of cultural capital elaborates forms of cultural capital, while noting the contested, reciprocal, historical, and constructed nature of cultural capital, a dually subjective and objective phenomenon. He wrote:

Cultural capital can exist in three forms: in the *embodied* state, i.e., in the form of long-lasting dispositions of the mind and body; in the *objectified* state, in the form of cultural goods (pictures, books, dictionaries, instruments, machines, etc.), which are the trace or realization of theories or critiques of these theories, problematic, etc.; and in the *institutionalized* state, a form of objectification which must be set apart because, as will be seen in the case of educational qualifications, it confers entirely original properties on the cultural capital which it is presumed to guarantee. (Bourdieu, 1986, p. 241)

In the end, there is separation of the qualifications *as institutional certification* from the cultural goods, problematics, and dispositions that are the substance of cultural capital. So much of the research about the effects of mentoring assume the institutional markers are how we measure success. This is where Bourdieu would say research all too often mistakes the marker for the substance that begets the marker. It is also why Bourdieu is less sanguine about the prospects of institutionalized schooling altering who has what cultural capital. For him the school is primarily about certification of the cultural capital that is valued by the dominant group.

Bourdieu also has an expansive view of social capital that cannot be reduced to a simple objectification. Social capital is actual and potential, material and symbolic, of varying durability, based in recognition, situated in group membership, and constituted in 'institutioning acts" in which interpretation plays back onto cultural production. He explains:

CLASS CROSSINGS

> Social capital is the aggregate of the actual or potential resources which are linked to possession of a durable network of more or less institutionalized relationships of mutual acquaintance and recognition—or in other words, to membership in a group—which provides each of its members with the backing of the collectivity-owned capital, a "credential" which entitles them to credit, in the various senses of the word. These relationships may exist only in the practical state, in material and/or symbolic exchanges which help to maintain them. They may also be socially instituted and guaranteed by the application of a common name (the name of a family, a class, or a tribe or of a school, a party, etc.) and by a whole set of instituting acts designed simultaneously to form and inform those who undergo them; in this case, they are more or less really enacted and so maintained and reinforced, in exchanges. Being based on indissolubly material and symbolic exchanges, the establishment and maintenance of which presuppose reacknowledgment of proximity, they are also partially irreducible to objective relations of proximity in physical (geographical) space or even in economic and social space. (Bourdieu, 1986, pp. 248–249)

Social capital thus is never reducible to material social network membership, as important as that may be. Social capital is about recognition of membership and what can be built with it.

Much of the research that uses cultural and social capital ends up focusing on an objectified view of each. This same research then misses Bourdieu's fundamental point that these forms of capital only have value on the particular *field* of social endeavor. The capitals of the 'street' are valued on that field but not necessarily on the field of formal education. Yosso (2005) argues that many researchers misunderstand, and therefore misuse, Bourdieu on these points. She argues they do not problematize what forms of capitals are valued in which field, thus underestimating the knowledge and capabilities of less powerful groups.

For Bourdieu, social, cultural and symbolic capital are masked forms of economic capital. He writes:

> So it has to be posited simultaneously that economic capital is at the root of all the other types of capital and that these transformed, disguised forms of economic capital, never entirely reducible to that definition, produce their most specific effects only to the extent that they conceal (not least from their possessors) the fact that economic capital is at their root, in other words-but only in the last analysis-at the root of their effects. (Bourdieu, 1968, p. 252)

Bourdieu then points us not to measures of forms of capital but to the conversions between economic capital and other forms of capital:

> The convertibility of the different types of capital is the basis of the strategies aimed at ensuring the reproduction of capital (and the position occupied in social space) by means of the conversions least costly in terms of conversion work and of the losses inherent in the conversion itself (in a given state of the social power relations). The different types of capital can be distinguished according to their reproducibility or, more precisely, according to how easily they are transmitted i.e., with more or less loss and with more or less concealment; the rate of loss and the degree of concealment tend to vary in inverse ratio. Everything which helps to disguise the economic aspect also tends to increase the risk of loss (particularly the intergenerational transfers). Thus the (apparent) incommensurability of the different types of capital introduces a high degree of uncertainty into all transactions between holders of different types. (Bourdieu, 1986, pp. 253–254)

Unfortunately, many who have picked up this distinction tend to focus on a subset of these capitals and miss or ignore Bourdieu's admonishment that the real significance is not in the forms per say but in their transformation.

This understanding of class is not prevalent in mentoring research. Rather than class being seen as a variable, Bourdieu sees it as a set of capitals that all have dynamics built around the dominance of economics. Mentoring research then uses class as a variable to explain or predict the outcomes of mentoring, but we think it is advantageous to think of mentoring a way of 'doing class' itself. Mentoring may be productively seen as a class dynamic itself.

## 5 Social Class as a Strategy of Dominance

There is a tendency to think of social class as a social structure. This thinking has many points in its favor. First, thinking of class as a structure emphasizes a minimally 'fixed' nature, solid and unchanging. There is permanence to its presence. It is not as much negotiable as something that must be negotiated with. Second, class as a structure implies an arrangement of forces and materials in relation to one another. In class theory, this arrangement is hierarchical—often lower to upper. Third, thinking of class as a structure tends to see arrangement as involving allocation—the lower has less (and/or different)

CLASS CROSSINGS

than the middle and the middle has less and/or different than the upper class. Fourth, class in this way of thinking is an agent, and people are subject to its agency. We belong to a class and a class has characteristics that we assume as individuals. We may be more than our social class but we are at base our class. Fifth and related, social class as structure also promotes a feeling of inevitability. Class exists. It is present and immutable. It organizes social life in ways that benefit some over others.

Thinking of social class as a structure also has some history, often reduced to the Marxist notion that the class structure must be overthrown. The idea that revolution followed by a dictatorship of the proletariat is at base a reification of the idea that class is a structure. Class is so stolid that it can be undercut only by itself—it contains the seeds of its own destruction rather than there being dynamics at play. Of course, most analysts now would argue that Marx was wrong in his prophesy of revolution but thinking of class as a structure is dominant. In this, the Right is as bound as the Left. When some wished to assign blame to larger capitalist institutions for the post-2008 economic recession, those on the Right decried this as promoting "class warfare." Regardless on one's partisan political stand, the point here is that the 'war' image reproduces the structural view of social class. The fear of class warfare is the fear that revolution, war, is the only option to redress social class differences.

Class-as-structure is literally dehumanizing but it also works to deflect blame from wealthy capitalists themselves. In this way of thinking, the upper classes may be benefitting but it is because of the inevitable, immutable structure—not because they act to garner and preserve their class advantages. This in turn gets tied to notions of social mobility. The agentic motif of class-as-structure is the idea of meritocracy. Here the class structure rewards effort and talent with social mobility. Those in the upper class deserve their status and wealth because meritocracy is at work.

Of course, there is much wrong with the class as structure way of thinking. For example, if it were in fact true then the cries against the 'death tax' (the misrepresentation of inheritance taxes for the very wealthy) would be nonsensical. The inheritor would simply lose the money because the structure rewards talent and effort not wealth itself. Moreover, there would be little change in wealth distribution due to changes in taxes. Yet it is evident that the tax changes during the Reagan administration and after led to increased centralization of wealth. Likewise, wage stagnation post 1970 and the shift to a post-industrial economy has shrunk the middle class sufficiently that some analysts see the end of the middle class (Noblit & Pink, 2016). (We will return to the implications of this later.) Unlike the class-as-structure way of thinking, social class is not immutable—it changes. Also, people are agents—at work taking advantage and avoiding blame. As E. P. Thompson (2001, p. 3) so famously put it: 'I do not see class as a 'structure,' nor even a 'category,' but as something which in fact happens (and can be shown to have happened) in human relationships."

If class-as-structure has so much wrong with it, then there must be some reason for its continuing dominance in both social theory and common parlance. Our argument is that it continues to hold sway because it has power behind it. It serves the interests of the powerful, working as a *strategy* of the wealthy to claim benefits and avoid responsibility for purposively stratifying people nationally and globally.

As a *strategy*, class-as-structure has worked rather well. O'Brien's (1999) analysis of class in antebellum Georgia, for example, shows how elites worked to create a white lower class that served to suppress African Americans. This class enforced Jim Crow more than law ever could. As a *strategy* of the Southern elites, this enabled both surplus labor and low wages. The white lower class focused on the threat African Americans were to their tenuous claim to what jobs there were, and created a fictive kinship of whiteness. There is a parallel in the debate over immigration in the United States. Similar to the late 19th and early 20th Century, immigration has been used by employers as a way to suppress wage growth and unionization. Today, businesses hire undocumented workers (and largely escape legal scrutiny) enabling wages to be suppressed for all. In shifting the blame to the immigrants for this economic practice, business owners create a *strategy* that makes working class whites a xenophobic force in politics. There are many more examples of how social class is better seen as a strategy than a structure but we have made our point for this paper. Thinking of class-as-structure is not merely a theoretical point of view. Rather it should be seen as *a strategy of the dominant classes* to deflect blame and responsibility for the consequences of accelerated capital accumulation.

Our argument is that mentors 'do class' to their mentees. It is a set of strategies of dominance. 'Doing class' becomes a pedagogy that denigrates as it provides an alternative. Yet as we will demonstrate the doing of class is primarily about changing the cultures of the youth. It is less about social and economic capital and the only transformation of cultural capital it suggests is a faith in education. The Gold Medal program adds services and elements that more effect a transformation but in the end it too is limited to cultural capital in its objectified form—educational credentials. Thus mentoring may be seen more a dynamic reproducing class differences than a process of social mobility.

## 6 Class Crossings

It is probably inevitable that mentors end up doing class to the mentees. Mentors are selected because they have something to offer to the youth. They also are volunteers—meaning in part that they wish to 'do good.' There are deep resonances in each of these positionings. The program is, of course, all about school completion and college going and so they seek mentors who both can model, and have knowledge, about college going. The mentors in 'doing good' of course position themselves as worthy and capable of helping others—key tenets of white privilege and middle and upper class philanthropy and service. Such positioning of course frame those they are working with in certain ways as well. The mentoring relationships in a successful mentoring program are largely centered on social class mobility. As one of the women mentors put it:

> I just want to see her achieve the goals that she has now, in terms of, um, finishing college and, um, you know, pursuing nursing which is … is … could be her career goal at this time. And I think, um, I just also want to see her achieve a higher standard of living than where she came from. Um … and I think she will. Um … and I guess I just, um, you know, want to continue to be, um, just a support … just a support for her and continue to be proud of what she's accomplishing and continue to be involved in her with how school's going and all that kind of stuff.

One can be picky here and note that the mentors' pride connotes a form of ownership of the mentees' successes. We can also see that the mentors' desires for the mentee drive part of her involvement, and 'support' indicates that the mentor has sufficient 'capital' to provide resources to the mentee. All of these signal the professional, middle class status of mentor and the lower class status of the mentee. Yet, of course, this is why the mentoring program exists—to attempt to develop a transference from higher status mentors to lower status mentees. As another mentor put it: "I grew up with a lot of privilege being part of the university community, and really good schools here, and being with family—and being with my family who likes to travel, and my dad whose work takes him all around the world, so that, those are important factors." Mentoring thus is about class stratification in key ways. The satisfaction of the mentors with their role is embedded in the mentees fulfilling the desires of the mentors. As a very enthusiastic mentor put it: "I can easily categorize this as one of the most fulfilling experiences I have had as an adult. In terms of feeling like I am making an impact, that she really values what I have to contribute, so it has been wonderful."

## 7 Mentors 'Doing Class'

The mentors 'do class' in very particular ways. Using Bourdieu's theory of capital enables us to interpret what they do and what limits there are in what they do. The mentors do provide economic, social and cultural capital but emphasize one form more than the others. We will argue that this way of doing class crossings is in fact a 'double cross.' It asks mentees to accept symbolic violence in exchange for social mobility and then it fails to deliver on this promise. Following Bourdieu, efforts to subjugate or replace one's cultural heritage with another (via assimilation, acculturation, education, etc.) is always symbolic violence.

### 7.1 *Economic Capital*

There is evidence of mentors working on the three primary forms of capital (symbolic capital will not be separated out below as it is contained in all the representations the mentors offered). Sometimes the mentors worked directly on economic capital. A husband of a mentor (they were interviewed together) speaks of the direct economic capital his wife provides to the mentees family:

> (my wife) does a really effective job of finding resources for them, so you know, whether it's through sort of small pots of resources, whether it's from the church or scholarship programs, or grants, or sort of programs combines a lot of those to provide them with resources so that they can have a computer and have a computer, and have internet, and have lots of books at home, and such as that.

Another mentor had hung in with her mentee for many years, surviving both geographic moves and relational difficulties. After the mentee had graduated from high school, this mentor found that directly addressing economic capital was required. In the quote below, the mentor both takes responsibility for addressing the economic issue but in acknowledging she has had similar concerns displays a superiority as well:

> ... she had an issue where she had some money that she owed to, um, the college that she had gone to for part of a semester and, um, she didn't know about it for a long time or something. It's something she thought had been paid off by a scholarship that she had. And so it came up as an issue now because she was going to be trying to transfer to a four-year college and she had to have that transferred release. And so that ... so she had ... she didn't know how to take care of it financially, she

CLASS CROSSINGS

didn't have the resources to do it and I think she was sort of avoiding or evading the issue, um, for a little while. And so, um, I … she mentioned this to me when I was home visiting, um, maybe last year sometime and I sort of said, "Okay, well look. I've done this kind of thing before too where I haven't made the smartest financial management decisions but you've just got to face it and figure out what it is and how you're gonna take care of it; otherwise it's gonna keep you from accomplishing your goals.

Another economic capital move was creating linking school grades to monetary rewards:

I even, just to encourage him to do well in school because I needed something to get him going, I um, I'd attach a dollar value to each grade. So I'd say, "(Mentee), you know, for an A it's this much." Only for A's, B's, and C's. And I would actually subtract, I think I subtracted money. So he'd get like $20 for an A, you know, $10 for a B, and -$10 for a C, maybe $10 for a B, but anyway, so I did that a couple of times, and that seemed to get his attention, so I was like, Ok. And it wasn't a lot, but it was enough to give him some pocket money. And I'm trying to make the association with him that if you do well in school, for later in your life, it can translate into dollars and cents.

In all these, the mentors are working economic capital and linking education to economic mobility. In all, however, there were very few incidents of such linkages in the mentor interviews. Moreover, at least one mentor was put off by the explicitness of mentees about their desire for direct economic capital:

I was really off-put because she learned from a girl older than she is in Gold Medal that she should go to the Counseling Office and ask for a mentor. "They take you places and spend money on you." So when she said that to me, that's when I felt like, well … you know, I don't think that I want to be in somebody's life for that reason.

## 7.2    *Social Capital*

Social capital was also rarely referred to by mentors. In the interviews, mentors would most often discuss social capital in terms of introducing the mentee to the mentor's immediate family. This is clearly important and can be transformed into economic capital as explained by one mentor:

(my family) probably had a little bit of a benefit to her in terms of a professional connection, because, I mean, she now works as a nurse's assistant in the hospital where my father works and my ... my mother does public health work and has ... both of my parents have run into her at the hospital. So she's, you know ... she's known them and she's run into them.

Yet few said they were directly linking their mentee to others who would enable the social connections that lead to opportunities for social mobility. One mentor, who saw her efforts as limited, was nevertheless a clear exception to this when she said:

So I've introduced her to a lot of professionals. Any time I have an opportunity for someone that has an occupation that I thought that she didn't know about or ... that's pretty much probably about it.

As important as this mentor's actions no doubt were, it should be noted that they fall short of Bourdieu's criteria for social capital as recognition of membership in the group.

### 7.3    *'Doing Class' through Cultural Capital*

As noted earlier, Bourdieu saw cultural capital as primarily developed through families. For Bourdieu, cultural capital is largely implicit, deeply coded into youth through their earliest and most intimate relations. He was less than sanguine about cultural capital being developed through secondary relations and social institutions. He saw educational credentials for example as the institutionalized state of cultural capital—not as embodied dispositions that make class standings 'natural' and 'obvious' to observers.

In efforts to provide cultural capital, the mentors worked on changing the youth to fit the stratified economic system. For Bourdieu (1977), this effort to replace one's home culture with a different culture as a form of symbolic violence where one's family is devalued, where the cultural capital of the family is devalued, and where social power is exercised to make this transition. Again, one might argue this a reality of class mobility—except given that the provision of social and economic capital by the mentors are so decidedly rare in the mentor interviews. The result, we argue, is that the class work done by the mentors is primarily cultural assimilation and only indirectly related to social mobility—rather it is linked to the myth of mobility. As Meyer (1994) has argued, education has the status of a faith belief in our globalized society, even though social class mobility is quite low in the U.S. (Barry, 2005). The mentors primarily focus on changing the culture of the mentee. They provide

CLASS CROSSINGS 77

little social or economic capital and there is no evidence that they tell the mentees about the low probability of class mobility in the U.S. Whether ignorant or intentional, this can be read, following the Brantlinger (2003) quoted earlier, as dominance for its own end—making the lower class believe the values of middle and upper classes are the 'right' ones.

The mentors perform class dominance well. As we will show, they both teach the cultural capital of the upper classes and denigrate the capital of the mentees' families almost in the same moment. They do this by emphasizing the values of 'hard work,' of higher education, of self-confidence, of individual will, of responsibility, and 'good choices'—all in the service of faith in education to alter class position. The mentors then enforce compliance through their mentoring relationship. As one mentor put it: "... to keep her on the right path" or alternatively phrased as a problem, "I wouldn't call them rough spots, but you know, when he kinda doesn't listen as much ...." Fear is also used, as one mentor recounts:

> He (the mentee) says, you know, these people were, you know, they had drugs on them, and you know, we talked about that and I said, "you don't want to be smoking, you don't want to be doing drugs of any kind" and I think the things that's working with him is, you know, I said to (the mentee) "if you want to be an athlete, you know, if you want to play professional basketball, you can't be doing drugs." That's what I did. I liked ice hockey, so I said athletes don't do this kind of stuff. I said it will affect your development. I think that's another thing that resonated, because he wants to be really tall. I said, "(Mentee), these drugs have all kinds of side effects, one of them could be your brain development, your physical development could be affected" and I think once he hears like he's not going to grow as tall or be as smart—Yeah, that kind of scared him enough to listen.

They also replace cultural capital though 'exposure' to the social institutions and experiences of the upper classes. The same mentor quoted above explains:

> Well, I'm just guessing, but I think he—we've probably just been able to expose him to things that he might not otherwise have had a chance to experience. So you know, so maybe he wouldn't have been able to go to a game in Greensboro, or um, just having me—actually he plays on the league in Chapel Hill—having me come to watch his games, you know, maybe that has some kind of positive effect. Maybe me playing basketball with him. Um, or I take him to play ice hockey. So I got him ice hockey,

you know, so he could experience ice hockey. We've taken him to the beach, you know, he'd never kind of been boogie boarding before so we got him out on the ocean. The water, he loves that. I took him for swimming lessons so he knows how to swim now, so I think maybe, and I feel like, you know he calls me out of the blue to get together, you know "Can we do something today?" So I don't know how to exactly describe what he's getting out of it ....

The mentor signals that 'exposure' is not material or instrumental. It will not change the income or the education status of the mentee. Without these, mentoring is about valuing cultural capital of the mentor's social class over that of the youth. This capital is of a particular form. Again it values hard work, self-confidence, individual will, responsibility and 'good choices' all in the service of higher education.

The mentors have a consistent message that presumes the students do not have the basic value of *hard work* for getting ahead in the U.S., and also assumes that assuming new values is not difficult: ... *Look, anybody can do this, you know, you just have to do well in school and continue to work hard, you know, it's not a big deal.* Hard work, according to the mentors, will lead to the youth being able to buy 'cool' things': ... *he'll talk about my car ... it's a cool car, whatever, and I'm like, ... you can have whatever car you want, but you know, no one is going to give it to you. You just have to work hard for it.* The mentors value the mentees' families by the degree the family embraces the hard work value important to the mentors, even as they indicate that the families are not all they could be. In the following, the mentors actually undercut their claim that hard work is the secret to getting ahead. Hard work counts only if it works financially and if it is accompanied with assimilation into white society:

> His mom's really um, you know, I think a good role model. She has worked hard, she just got a new job working in Durham as a social worker. She just moved into a modest, but nice home. They are very hardworking, both of her parents are housekeepers either at UNC or at Carolina Inn. So, they are very hardworking people but they really don't go much outside their peer or ethnic group.

Moreover, the cultural value of hard work is seen to emerge from *individual will*. As one mentor explained:

> You have to define your own potential. Your potential isn't defined by your parents. But at the same time it's not a level playing field and everyone

doesn't start at the same. Here there is a recognition of existing social stratification but, for mentors, it can be overcome through individual intention and action—and this is lacking for some of the mentees: ... she, you know, doesn't complete assignments .... Her frame of mind is such that she can't keep herself organized.

Another mentor linked individual will to *responsibility*:

> I think just in terms ... maybe some specific situations were just sort of teaching her about how to sort of take responsibility for her actions and also ... actually, we did a lot of ... there were a number of times where we did sort of tutoring as well or like, you know, getting her to work on her homework with me. And so I think that was probably good in terms of just like getting her ... giving her the sense of importance of focusing on her academics, which she wasn't always totally focused there.

The mentors teach the mentees that not taking individual responsibility has consequences that are undesirable. One mentor explains how he put it to his mentee:

> The only person you are hurting is you. You're gonna flunk, you're not gonna get a good grade and you're not, you know, get into (a coach's) acceptable set of people he would consider.

The mentors, though, ask more of the mentees than just avoiding consequences. The mentees are lauded when they take on the individual will and responsibility values as their own, making and being at ease with making *good choices: That's what's really important—that she feels good with her decisions and that she's ... she's okay with what she decided.*

Of course, this is the mentors' taken for granted world and the program itself tries to make the mentors aware of this and the privilege it entails. The mentors acknowledge this but nonetheless they are still do their culture as class to the mentees. In doing so, *self-confidence* rings through: *I worked really hard and I have really high expectations of myself and the, you know the, I definitely have to recognize sort of like the structure of privilege within which I can experience those challenges.* What the above mentor sees in herself, even with a recognition of the privilege that accompanies it, is reflected in what the mentees lack. As a mentor explains: ... *she doesn't always feel confident with who she is. Um ... and it's not confidence about how well she does in school or her character or anything.* As a result of this deficit, the mentors work directly on confidence itself: *So certainly much of my, much of my pragmatic orientation is around giving him the skills and the confidence to achieve that goal. Um, you know, 'cause the career part, what career he does doesn't matter to me, but you know I think that for the most part to be successful in almost any career he mentions like doing higher education is important, um, and ah, anyway, and then to be an effective member of society in all of these respects that we've touched on.*

The mentors then have a pedagogy of class that focuses on the values of hard work, individual will and responsibility, confidence and good choices. These values mark the mentors as belonging to a professional class position and they teach them as cultural capital for the mentees. However, just having the values is not enough—one has to have them in an 'embodied' form, as Bourdieu puts it. In this regard, the mentors also teach both how to act as well as speak in ways that signal middle class status. Such middle class comportment includes greeting and address behavior, handshaking, eye contact, listening, and politeness. The mentor explains:

> I hope I've helped in small ways like when he meets with adults, he's not sure how to greet them. He's kind of shy, he's not sure if he should shake their hand, he doesn't speak up very much. I've said (mentee) when you meet somebody, I say you know shake their hand say it's a pleasure to meet you Mr. so and so or Mrs. So and so, my name is you know. Um little thing like how you would greet somebody. I already talked to him about looking folks in the eye when you are meeting and talking to them. And listening to them. And be sure to say thank you when folks do something for you. And let me say that I only had to say that once and never did I have to say it to (a later mentee). I think (current mentee) probably explained to Jose that when we get through or do something that is neat you say thank you. But 'how do you do? It's nice to meet you.' It's not just the head down and we don't acknowledge the person. Eye contact, 'how do you do? It's nice to meet you?' and she said, "Okay, okay, okay."

All of these are about signaling one's equality to those being met, one's belonging to the middle class in this case. However, the lower classes have a history of being punished for such hubris. Required deference is the rule that has been enforced historically on the mentees' families, and thus the mentors actively place the mentees *between classes* by expecting such comportment. The mentees are expected to choose to violate the classed norms of relation that their families have had taught them—and to behave as if they belong to the middle class. The mentees then are asked to situate themselves betwixt and between

CLASS CROSSINGS

the social class of their families and the social class of their mentors. They are expected by the mentor to leave their family behind.

Mentors also enforce appropriate language use as part of comportment. The specifics vary by the mentee's racialized group but the enforcement seems similar. One mentor who works with an African American mentee explained about promoting code switching:

> I guess that maybe one interesting anecdote is um, with regards to language. Because I do find myself, find myself looking for opportunities to correct his language when we're talking together and he uses language, language that isn't formally, ah, ah, formally grammatical, uh, or you know sort of, significant non-standard pronunciation, and I guess that with regards to that, I'd like him to not feel like, and I think like I'm particularly cautious, I don't usually correct him when it's just a matter of pronunciation or even sort of, you know, casual speech, but if it's something outstanding or you know, particularly if it's sort of an attempt to make sort of a more formal comment but he uses less formal language then I correct him and I guess that I'd like for him to do there, recognizing that class and race and uh, class and race and social settings play a big role in language, um, is to know that, that uh, that's it's ok to use different forms of language but to sort of recognize when you use different forms of language, um, so you know, like, that's definitely a personal take on it. But ah, but I'm aware that that's sort of a more difficult issue for me to solve, to approach.

Another mentor works with a Latina:

> I would say the one thing that I work with her on more than probably anyone, because I do speak perfect English and ... and I'm ... I'm around her often, is I work on her ... her language skills. I have her read to me often. I tell her that if, you know, she comes to a word and she doesn't know what it means, even if she doesn't know it's a stop for her, she needs to stop. I bought her a little dictionary. "You need to look up that word and understand at least basically what that word means so you can go on." I think if I've helped her with anything, it's probably been her language skills.

All of this, of course, are forms of Bourdieu's (1977, p. 32) "symbolic violence" in which one replaces one's home cultural capital with another class's cultural capital. This is violence for Bourdieu because the home culture is being attacked. One mentor justifies this replacement of cultural capital by denigrating the class position of her mentee's mother's while portraying the mentor's experience as preferred to the extent of it being 'natural':

> Like I do think ... you know, I think that, um, I guess I feel sort of like, you know, her own, um, mother had, you know, has a lot of struggles ... has had a lot of struggles in life and hasn't necessarily been able to, um, provide for (mentee) probably as much as she's wanted to or ... or you know .... Sometimes I would just notice things like even going out to a restaurant that it wasn't actually second nature to (mentee) to necessarily do that 'cause it wasn't necessarily something that her family did. And so just kind of the ... how to sort of interact in that environment, it was just like ... and just ordering food at a restaurant and dealing with that situation was sometimes kind of a new experience, it seemed like.

The cultural capital of the professional middle classes links individual attributes to the person's success in life. For the professional middle classes, success is not just inherited. It is certified by education. Thus the mentors tend to focus on orienting the mentees to a *faith in education*. The mentors see this as another deficit in the families of the mentees. The deficit takes the form of both a lack of knowledge about how education works and a lack of commitment to their child's education, as the following accounts reveal:

> I'm flying solo a lot because they have no understanding of what it takes to succeed in high school, what it takes to get into college. It's been a lot of education. They do understand, of course, the benefit of a great high school education. So I must give them credit for that. They, you know, they really encourage (mentee), but they can't offer very much in the ways of guidance. I worry about, I don't think his mom takes (mentee)—and this is just a complete guess—but she doesn't take his academic success as seriously as I think she needs to. You know, she should have—forgo other things, and have an internet connection.

As noted above, mentors are recruited because they are assumed to have something to offer the child. A key part of this 'something' is the value they put on education:

... Like education is, from my world view ... education is the central means and activity to be successful and happy in life. And so, I think that ... the feeling that I get is that if he's successful in education the other things will follow. This

CLASS CROSSINGS

"reality" is a testimony to the mentors' own character and a taken for granted assumption that this faith in education will work out for everyone:

> I am very smart. I am good at teaching. I am pretty accepting of people. One of the things I like doing with (mentee) is explaining to her how the world works. You know, times when she has been infuriated in her classes, I have said "if you ... if the teacher believes that you are interested in what's going on, then she is going to cut you more slack than if you act out" and that is sort of just money in the bank. If your teacher asks questions and you are involved, that is going to come in handy if you have hard times in that class and stuff like that. Why people behave the way they do. I have a lot of interest in that and I feel like those are kind of the keys to the world.

The mentoring program expects the mentors to advocate for the youth and in the vein of their faith in education they do so. Yet in doing so they also confirm the mentee's social class deficits that they use to justify their roles as mentors. Advocacy is often seen as a positive thing to be done for the less enfranchised but in the below, advocacy also reinscribes the deficits seen in the mentees' cultural capital:

> ... when she got the low grade in Science, um, I asked her why, we talked about it. I emailed her Science teacher and I told him that she's ... he's using words that she doesn't understand and she's embarrassed to raise her hand. So could ... I know he's very busy, but could he work out something where he could just check in on her every once in a while and just get some eye contact as to whether she was confused, troubled, struggling.

In the above quote, it is apparent that the mentor has a form of deference for the teacher—as a member of the professional middle class and a keeper of the faith in education. Thus the mentors' advocacy can be quite different from that of some parents who see the school as systematic denying the child an education. As one mentor explained:

> I find even um, the parent-teacher meetings I've been to, um, a lot of times, the teacher—I think the teachers are in some way afraid of her. You know, it's like they are afraid to say anything negative because it's like she's going to be defensive of (mentee). Whereas it's not, if the teachers have something, they shouldn't be afraid to say something that's not, that's negative, if it's negative, it's negative, you know, you just have to

deal with it. But I think she's very protective, you know, I don't blame her for any of that, that's all natural parenting, you know, motherly instincts. You don't want to hear your son, anyone say anything negative, but if they're saying it in a constructive way, then they're saying it to help, you know. But she and I get along great, she's thanked me a million times for all that I do, which is nice to hear. Um, you know, I really, I—we have a good, a great ... as good of a relationship as I think we can have.

### 7.4  Mentor's Understanding of Their Class Position

The mentors of course recognize that they placed in classed position when doing mentoring. They understand that mentoring is asking them to 'do class' to the mentees:

> if anything, I would just maybe say just the, um, just the ... you know, the opportunity to be a role model to somebody that's pursuing a professional career and the work that's involved in doing that, I think it might have been beneficial for her to have that as a role model.

The mentors also understand how identity can be comprised in this: It's very difficult to maintain your cultural and social identity when you're trying to fit into the community around you. But even with this, GOLD MEDAL mentors see 'doing class' as appropriate and necessary. Symbolic violence is justified by the myth of social mobility.

### 8  Conclusion

Class is all about money—and using money as the justification of status. Money and status are objects of desire—driving the interest in social mobility. The GOLD MEDAL mentors are both products of this logic and participants in its reproduction. They are not villains in any obvious way. They are giving, caring and attentive to the youth they serve. The program explicitly talks with them about privilege, inequality, and their role as mentors. In the quotes above we witness their awareness. Yet awareness is not enough to overcome their complicity with stratification. There is no evidence that they perceive the possibility of a society without significant stratification. They act not to equalize society but rather to sponsor individual social mobility. This is not to assign blame to them. Rather it points out how youth mentoring as a social formation is situated.

Youth mentoring is in essence an ameliorating phenomenon. The mentors are caught up in the social formation that is mentoring, and that social formation assumes stratification is 'reality.' Youth mentoring assumes that the goal is to overcome the mentee's origins and experiences and replace them with more valued perspectives, orientations and dispositions. It is mentoring that assumes the youth must fit an unfair social order. GOLD MEDAL, to its merit, is actually more explicit about race and inequality than many programs. It also pushes advocacy more than other programs. GOLD MEDAL's staff are clear they are working against social stratification, and working against the social form of mentoring. Yet GOLD MEDAL too is situated as ameliorative. Mentoring is sorely lacking in the face of systems and beliefs that enact stratification. This is a key reason GOLD MEDAL has developed a wide range of services—to overcome the limitations of youth mentoring.

In the preceding, we see what the program is working against. For all the good intentions and efforts of mentors, they inscribe their class on the youth. It is clear that their class position has brought the mentors many benefits and they wish their mentees to have similar advantages. It is in this wish that they 'do class' to the youth. Yet they 'do class' in a particular way. The program and the mentors deemphasize direct provision of economic capital in favor of developing relationships with the mentees built more around being together and sharing common interests. The mentors also provide little direct social capital, outside of family to family relations. Instead, the mentors 'do class' primarily through cultural capital emphasizing values of 'hard work,' of higher education, of self-confidence, of individual will, responsibility, and 'good choices'—all in the service of a faith that education will alter class position. The push is for these values to become "second nature" to the youth. We have shown that this way of 'doing class' comes at a price. To promote these values, the mentors construct the mentees families as deficient. All too often assertions of family strengths are accompanied by denigration. These can be seen as instances of Bourdieu's (1977, p. 32) "symbolic violence."

Some may argue that realistically this is the only way to 'do class' for these youth, that the violence is justified by the outcome. The evaluation on which this book is built provides some evidence for this view. GOLD MEDAL mentees get better grades than a matched group of students, graduate at a higher rate than the district as a whole, and almost all go to college. Clearly, it can be argued that ends justify the means.

However, there is another reality that counters this. Mentoring buys the myths of meritocracy and of social mobility. Meritocracy is the underpinning of the professional middle class. It assumes that the values promoted above will lead to social mobility. However, there is considerable evidence that meritocracy is a myth. Instead, it can be argued that favoritism as a social practice better explains social reproduction and social mobility (Asma, 2012).

Moreover, mentoring assumes that mobility is a reasonable goal in our society. For all the Horatio Alger stories, however, the U.S. has the least social mobility of industrialized nations (Barry, 2005). The middle class has been shrinking over time. The professional middle class that the mentors represent is no longer able to absorb those who desire mobility. Indeed, when these mentors leave the workforce at the end of their careers, their social class will likely exit with them. The middle class is all but void.

Mentoring, we argue, should rethink its logic. The mentoring relationship remains important and significant to both mentor and mentee. However, there may be better ways of 'doing class' than we see here. We would argue that mentoring can be resituated as a process to reduce inequality. This would be based first in efforts that attack social policies that stratify—tax systems, corporate welfare, and so on. This, of course, politicizes mentoring and no doubt will have political consequences that proponents may be unwilling to accept. We think these concerns are shortsighted but we do acknowledge that funding for mentoring is tied to accepting the myths above.

Even if mentoring programs do not choose to go on the offensive for social equality, the data here suggest there are ways to rethink mentoring in productive ways. First, mentoring can rethink how economic capital can be directly exchanged. Even if mentors do not have significant capital to transfer to mentees, there are many ways to provide incidental funds that help youth. Our data demonstrate that mentors do provide such funds for summer programs, athletic teams, and club participation. These can be emphasized. They can also be understood as directly affecting social capital and thus mentoring programs can identify and vet such opportunities for such benefits. We think it is also reasonable to rethink how mentors can create employment for mentees. There clearly must be a concern about exploitation that guides such efforts, but there are models of youth business creation and entrepreneurship that may be worth considering. Mentors can do more about developing economic capital than is currently the case in mentoring programs.

The extent to which it is helpful to think of social mobility as being based in favoritism then mentoring should more explicitly emphasize social capital. Mentors should seek ways for their mentees to meet and associate with others who may prove useful in later life. Social capital is an investment over time and needs nurturing and development. As our social class system collapses into what appears to be 2 classes—wealthy and working or leading and dependent—then new ideas and social practices are needed to guide how we to be together in the new working class. New ways of reaching across age, race, education, community, and beliefs will need to be developed. Mentoring programs can be situated to facilitate this.

Finally, cultural capital is a chimera in all this. The myth of mobility cannot justify symbolic violence. Beliefs and practices have histories and strengths untold. Sharing rather than replacing seems to be a more productive way of working with cultural capital. Mentoring programs can be places of cultural and social expression and production. As GOLD MEDAL has learned, there is much the arts can do to build identities that resist denigration and enhance engagement. Mentoring can resituate itself as a forum of cultural production—sustaining strengths and changing to more effectively address stratification. We think the effort must be to develop mechanisms for social and cultural capital to be converted into economic capital, as Bourdieu emphasized.

Mentoring has been all about crossing classes but we have demonstrated that it can be seen as a 'double cross.' The mentees are asked to give their home cultures with the promise of mobility precisely when mobility no longer characterizes American society. What is needed now is concerted work on class construction. What is to be the character of the permanent working class? What is the relation of this class to the elite class? As the other chapters in this book highlight, this class construction must be intersectional. Race, gender, sexual orientation, age, ability and social class are all at play in stratification and consequently in mentoring programs. We need to foster all of these crossings since class crossings are no longer realistically possible.

### References

Asma, S. (2012). In defense of favoritism. *The Chronicle of Higher Education.* http://chronicle.com/article/In-Defense-of-Favoritism/135610/

Barry, B. (2005). *Why social justice matters*. Malden, MA: Polity Press.

Bourdieu, P., & Passeron, J. (1977). *Reproduction in education, society and culture*. Newbury Park, CA: Sage Publications.

Bourdieu, P. (1986). The forms of capital. In J. Richardson (Ed.), *Handbook of the theory and research in the sociology of education* (pp. 241–258). New York, NY: Greenwood Press.

Brantlinger, E. (2003). *Dividing classes: How the middle class negotiates and rationalizes school advantage.* New York, NY: Routledge.

Castagno, A., & Brayboy, B. (2008). Culturally responsive schooling for indigenous youth: A review of the literature. *Review of Educational Research, 78*(4), 941–993.

Crenshaw, K. (1995). Mapping the margins: Intersectionality, identity politics, and violence against women of color. In K. Crenshaw, N, Gotanda, G. Peller, & K. Thomas (Eds.), *Critical race theory.* New York, NY: New Press.

Delpit, L. (1988). The silenced dialogue: Power and pedagogy in educating other people's children. *Harvard Educational Review, 58*(3), 280–298.

Deutch, N., Lawrence, E., & Henneberger, A. (2014). Social class. In D. Dubois & M. Karcher (Eds.), *Handbook of youth mentoring* (2nd ed., pp. 175–187). Los Angeles, CA: Sage Publications.

Dubois, D., & Karcher, M. (Eds.). (2014). *Handbook of youth mentoring* (2nd ed.). Los Angeles, CA: Sage Publications.

Ladson-Billings, G. (1995). Toward a culturally relevant pedagogy. *American Educational Research Journal, 32*(3), 465–491.

Marx, K. (1867). *Das Kapital.* Hamburg: Otto Meissner.

Meyer, J. (1994). The evolution of modern stratification systems. In D. Grusky (Ed.), *Social stratification* (pp. 730–738). Boulder, CO: Westview Press.

Moll, L., Soto-Santiago, S., & Schwartz, L. (2013). Funds of knowledge in changing communities. In K. Hall, T. Cremin, B. Comber, & L. Moll (Eds.), *International handbook of research on children's literacy, learning and culture.* New York, NY: Wiley.

Noblit, G., & Pink, W. (Eds.). (2016). *Education, equity and economy: Crafting a new intersection.* New York, NY: Springer.

O'Brien, T. (1999). *The politics of race and schooling: Public education in Georgia, 1900–1961.* Lanham, MD: Lexington Books.

Thompson, D. (Ed.). (2001). *The essential E. P. Thompson.* New York, NY: New Press.

Yosso, T. (2005). Whose culture has capital? A critical race theory discussion of community cultural wealth. *Race, Ethnicity, and Education, 8*(1), 69–91.

CHAPTER 4

# "I Don't Think It's Changed Me, It's Helped Mold Me": The Agency of Students of Color in a Whitestream Mentoring Organization

*Tim Conder and Alison LaGarry*

## 1　Introduction

In the above quote, former mentee Kayli, an African-American woman, described the impact of a school-sponsored mentoring program for students of color on her personal identity. Her word choice is telling; she deliberately makes clear that she claims space for her own identity in the process of being mentored. Yes, there are things that she has learned from her white mentor, Amy, but Kayli noted throughout her interview that she is careful to filter advice through her own personal "situation" or lens. Holland et al. (2008) stated that agency has traditionally been defined as "the socially mediated capacity of an actor to make a difference in, if not on, a social world" (p. 2). In the same paper, they posited that agency might be better conceptualized as "an emergent property of the coming together of history-in-person with a historically specific set of institutions and practices" (Holland et al., 2008, p. 2). We believe Kayli's steadfast claim speaks volumes about the identities and agency of students navigating the social complexities of participation in various spheres of social practice or figured worlds (Holland, Lachicotte, Skinner, & Cain, 1998). Specifically, we see Kayli's identity—her history-in-person, her identity formed in the wake of historical socio-cultural racial struggles and within the distinct local space of a whitestream mentoring program—not mediating agentic practice within a white-normed space or 'figured world of Whiteness.' In whole, we take away an impression of agency and self-authoring in the mentorship program that maintains a vision of mentees as agentic actors, even in the face of the pervasive and constraining "assumed normal" of whiteness.

For the purposes of this chapter, we will use the social practice theory of identity and agency, as described by Holland, Lachicotte, Skinner, and Cain (1998), as a frame with which to analyze interview data. Through the use of Extended Case Methodology (ECM) (Tavory & Timmermans, 2009) we seek to show that despite significant evidence that the mentorship program studied works to recruit mentees into a figured world of whiteness, participants

© KONINKLIJKE BRILL NV, LEIDEN, 2019 | DOI: 10.1163/9789004407985_005

still show distinct marks of agency. We concur with Holland et al. (1998) that identity formation is complex, multi-faceted, and is ongoing—always in a state of "becoming." As such, identity is formed through the interaction and overlapping of various contexts including—but not limited to—figured worlds, positional identities, self-authoring, and the interaction of enduring struggles within the contentions of local spaces of practice (History-In-Person). We, the authors, agree with Holland and colleagues who theorized agency as deeply aligned with identity, most clearly in "intimate identities," described by Mead (1912) as "I" and referring to an individual's inner consciousness. In the process of "becoming," actors are in a constant state of dialogism in which they are addressed ("me") and answering ("I") (Bakhtin, 1981). The meaning constructed by *answering* the varying voices of culture becomes an act of self-authoring. In our analysis of the mentoring program, we found that participants made significant forthright statements or "answers" regarding intimate identity.

Mentoring relationships, in the case of the mentoring program, involve engagement with persons of different races, ages, social classes, interests, and networks. In the mentoring program, mentees are typically students of color. Mentors in the program, though not entirely, are White persons drawn from a highly educated and upper income university community. Despite the additional unbalanced power dynamic that can be natural to any mentoring relationship, we have much evidence of students constructing powerful agentic identities despite the many challenges of position. One might think that mentee agency would get lost in the myriad of paths and expectations. But, in many cases, they seem to know 'where to go' and hence 'find their way.' In short student agency survives the enveloping, recruiting power of Whiteness.

## 2    Forming Identities in Practice

This chapter concentrates on the identities and agency among students of color in a primarily White school system and especially as participants in a primarily White interventionist mentoring organization. It has been demonstrated in much educational literature, including this volume, that Whiteness can be expressed as a pervasive and colonizing "normal" in educational settings (Hytten & Warren, 2003; Marx, 2004). As we will describe shortly, Whiteness functions as a cultural world or *figured world* that powerfully constructs meaning and shapes identity as a dominant paradigm in our society. Given that Whiteness often functions as an 'assumed normal' and an implicit standard that can imply a deficit posture among students of color, it would be easy to posit that these students would express diminished agency in these whitestream systems and relationships. Instead, we found the opposite to be true. We found most of the students interviewed constructing identities with significant agency despite the pervasiveness of Whiteness among the mentors, the mentoring organization evaluated, the school system, and this relatively affluent White community.

As previously alluded to, these observations that we will expose and defend below are rooted in a practice theory of identity and agency expressed by Holland, Lachicotte, Skinner, and Cain (1998). Drawing generously and creatively from the works of the French sociologist and anthropologist, Pierre Bourdieu, Russian philosopher and semiotician, Mikhail Bakhtin, Russian psychologist, Lev Semyonovich Vygotsky, and the theoretical reflexivism of American pragmatist philosopher, George Herbert Mead, Holland et al. (1998) made two overarching assertions about identities and agency. First, they challenge a reductionism that asserts fixed and singular identities among persons. Second, they affirm the critical role played by practice, including dialogical practice, in shaping both identities and agency. This first essential meta-claim stands as a rebuttal of the "general 'Western' notion of identity that takes as its prototype, a coherent, unified, and originary subject" (Holland et al., 1998, p. 7). In other words, identities are constantly forming; humans are perpetually *becoming* rather than products of a static identity. In a second meta-claim, instead of a fixed and singular idea of identity, Holland et al. (1998) describe identities "as social products ... lived in and through activity and so must be conceptualized as they develop in practice" (p. 5). This emphasis on identities—in practice, in activity, formulating, and reformulating—is part of a significant rupture in the social sciences referred to as the metatheoretical shift to practice. The human work of becoming, forming identities and asserting agency, occurs in social environments and in local spaces of practice. These assertions have been essential for our analysis. As we begin to elaborate on the interview data, one will easily see students expressing both identities and agencies that develop in very different practice settings. These various places of practice and relationship will often be marked by differing types and styles of agency.

## 2.1 *Figured Worlds*

One of the most notable and valuable contributions to identity and agency by Holland and colleagues is their description of cultural worlds of meaning as *figured worlds*. Put most simply, figured worlds are horizons of meaning performed in local spaces of practice. These are frames of meaning that interpret characters, actors, and actions. They are imaginary, "as if" worlds (Holland et al., 1998, p. 52) but they are not abstractions and are "social realit[ies] that [live] within dispositions mediated by relations of power" (p. 60). In other words, they are not 'everywhere,' ethereal abstractions, but are materialized and made real in spaces of practice. Figured worlds can come into being through storytelling and other cultural assumptions. Persons are recruited or drawn into figured worlds. These cultural worlds are related to historical phenomena but also are developed by the work of their participants. "The potency of a figured world is in its practice and performance" (Holland, 2012). Hence, the realms of the imagined and specific sites of practice merge in this theorization to yield verdant spaces of identity formation.

Many educational scholars have punctuated their areas of research with figured worlds. Similar to our work in a White mentoring organization, Urrieta (2009) wrote about the figured worlds of chicana/o activism within the local spaces of whitestream schools. Hatt (2009) also wrote about the figured world of "smartness" in American schools powerfully operating as "a tool of control and social positioning" (p. 20) as "a process of ascribing social power defined along lines of class and race" (p. 2). Hence students, in the figured world of smartness evoked in the space of classrooms, are recruited to the utilitarian values of the white, neo-liberal economy and ascribed roles within this society (Hatt, 2009).

Figured worlds, like that of "smartness" in the previous example, become powerful actors in the local spaces of practice where identities and agencies are forged. In the classroom, according to Hatt (2009), "smartness" functions as a strongly present horizon of meaning in certain circumstances with which students must address, contend, and react. In our research, we consistently encountered a deeply entrenched figured world of whiteness that was evoked in the spaces of a mentoring organization, mentoring relationships, and families of color.

## 2.2 The Figured World of Whiteness

For this chapter, we locate *whiteness* as the set of dominant, hegemonic expectations for practice in specific spaces. These overarching and persistent expectations impose an 'assumed normal' that assigns the highest value to social performances associated with white racial norms. Put more concisely—we describe the figured world of whiteness as one that promotes and expects white supremacy. Whiteness, along with racism, must then be situated within a distinctly racial construct that acknowledges individual performative acts (Bettez, 2011; Warren, 2001), but also sees the discursive role of individuals within the ideological framework of race.

For the mentoring organization studied, we found that whiteness functions as a horizon of meaning for all involved. The figured world of whiteness is one of hierarchies and inequalities, where one sees identity being constructed and hardened around the assumptions of inequalities and deficits. In studying

I DON'T THINK IT'S CHANGED ME, IT'S HELPED MOLD ME          93

white pre-service teachers, for example, Marx (2004) noted that the teachers she studied were prone to consider people-of-color as lacking expected characteristics or disadvantaged using what Valencia (1997) terms "deficit thinking." As a result, they considered the "cultures, home languages, families, intelligence, and self-esteem of the children they tutored and the other people of color they discussed as sadly inhibited by extraordinary deficits" (p. 35). This is particularly salient in the organization studied when, as mentioned above, white mentors are paired with mentees who identify as persons-of-color. In framing white mentorship as a key factor in a mentee's future success, the mentoring organization reinforces a horizon of meaning that both produces and reproduces this deficit view of students. In the discussion sections below, we will highlight data from mentee interviews that illustrates the various expectations placed upon mentees in specific contextual spaces—or spaces of local practice. Some particular dimensions included within this set of expectations include communication practices, achievement narratives, and participation in sanctioned extracurricular activities. Each of these dimensions, then, contribute to white-normed cultural imaginaries such as exclusivity, achievement, smartness, and comportment.

In acknowledging the figured world of whiteness overlaying the mentoring organization studied, it is of particular interest to ask if there are spaces where the discourses and inequalities of whiteness can be resisted or at least minimized. Through our analysis of the available data, we believe that these spaces for agency do exist. In the sections below, we take up two key spaces to explore student agency, presenting them in a simple progression beginning with the space (the mentoring organization itself) where we observed the least opportunity for agency and moving to a second space (the mentoring relationship) where mentees felt more able to assert agency originating in their own sense of personal identity. Considering both spaces, we describe how and where mentees name, resist, and reject the discourses of whiteness. Finally, we must state that the figured world of whiteness is not unique to the mentoring organization. Our purpose in naming it here is to bring attention to a set of dominant expectations that are assumed to be normal and thus made invisible. Additionally, we seek to show that while hegemonic racial ideologies and discourses constrain the frames of meaning-making within the mentoring organization, there are significant spaces and opportunities where mentees can and do demonstrate agency.

### 2.3    *Positional Identities and the Histories the Produce Them*

Hatt's (2009) paper exposed a second critical context for identity formation that is intimately woven into figured worlds, positionality. Social status, race, gender and other positional identities may deny access to or determine the manner of one's entry into specific figured worlds (Holland et al., 1998; Urrieta, 2009). It is critical to realize that local spaces of practice are neither innocent nor placid. They, instead, are spaces of contention where durable positionalities matter, motives such as prestige or power are often at stake, and strong resistance to specific figured worlds may be present. In addition to these inevitable contentions, "activity predicated upon a figured world is never quite single, never quite pure" (Holland et al., 1998, p. 238). In a local space of practice, many figured worlds can bump up against each other and their presence has to be arbitrated by persons in some manner.

As is apparent from these quotes, in the White world of this mentoring organization, positional identities matter deeply in the formation of personal identities and agency that is derived from personal identity. Also extremely significant are the grand histories that forge various positionalities. Holland and Lave (2001) refer to these histories as *enduring struggles* explaining that "the significance of enduring struggles lies in their scope in time, space, and political-economic relations, and part lies in their life-and-death, indelible impact on everyday lives" (p. 22). With their inertial power from the past, historical structures and legacies both energize and restrain practices within local spaces. An aspect of the contentiousness of local spaces is that some enduring struggles silence and suppress other struggles such that "only one or a few emerge to stand as the important struggles (and identities)" (p. 25).

An essential fulcrum to this theory is the assertion that enduring struggles obviously and profoundly impact individual lives and intimate identities, *but they do not do so directly*. This impact is mediated in local spaces of practice. Also present in the local space of contentious practices are "complex mediations between intimate, interiorized practices of identity" (Holland & Lave, 2001, p. 20) and these historical enduring struggles. As we move later to the acts of self-authoring done by students in the midst of and sometimes despite their positional identities, these "intimate, interiorized practices" which Holland and Lave (2001) refer to as *history-in-person* will become prominent. As we continue, we will demonstrate student struggling with racial positions and histories, yet still successfully authoring intimate identities that yield unique forms of agency.

## 3 Methods and Perspectives

We locate our methodology for this chapter in the genre of extended case method (ECM). Tavory and Timmermans (2009) defined ECM as "a theoretically driven ethnography, or what can be called 'theorygraphy,' in which research activities aim to modify, exemplify, and develop existing theories" (p. 244). Burawoy (1998) elaborated further on ECM's use of existing theory explaining that the goal is a "more inclusive generality. We begin with our favorite theory but seek not confirmations but refutations that inspire us to deepen that theory. Instead of discovering grounded theory, we elaborate existing theory" (p. 16). In the sense of these definitions, our analysis with practice theories of identity and agency fits comfortably within an ECM approach. We believe that this theoretical trajectory provides a strong lens to explore and describe the identities and agency of students in this mentoring program. We also believe that this study extends the theory itself.

We realize that no theory is innocent. Every theoretical construct is forged from perspectives and biases nurtured in the experiences of theorists. This is equally true for those who use theory as the base of analysis. Hence, we readily acknowledge our own lack of innocence in the use of theory in this analysis. Though neither of us grew up in privileged backgrounds, we are White researchers who are examining the identities and agency of students of color. We do not share their experience of growing up in the margins of primarily White school systems in a primarily White community. We have listened intently to their recognition and often strong rejection of the expectations of failure for students outside the dominant paradigm based on the historical and local struggles of race in this specific community. But we realize that we did not face this same struggle in our own lives. Having personally interviewed some of the mentees in the evaluation of this mentoring organization, we are very thankful for the vulnerability of these students to speak so frankly and perceptively to ones who look like the hegemonic culture they struggle with and have entered their lives from the highly privileged positions of doctoral students and researchers. As you read our upcoming analysis, we sincerely hope that you feel that we have listened well and listened honestly given our own privilege.

In the analysis that follows, we will begin by elaboration, often using the words of the students, in the previously named two spaces of practice under the umbrella of the figured world of Whiteness, the interactions of the students with the mentoring organization and their personal mentoring relationships. In an additional data section, we also look directly at the assertions and personal affirmations made by these same students within the interviews for this project. These assertions and affirmations certainly acknowledge how the figured world of Whiteness is regularly evoked in spaces of the mentoring organization and in mentoring relationships, yet they also reflect a retained sense of everyday agency of students of color in this whitestream organization located in a primarily White university community.

## 4 First Space of Practice—The Mentoring Organization

The first space of practice we noted in the data, described in remarkable consistency among participants, is that of the formal mentoring organization (FMO). As will be discussed in more detail below, this consistency of description marks the strength of the cultural imaginaries produced and reproduced within this space of administration, gatekeeping, and surveillance. Notably, mentees described this space of practice as distinctly separate from that of individual mentoring relationships. We assert that this space of practice serves to ensure the potency and strength of narratives within a figured world of whiteness. As Holland (2012) stated, the strength of a figured world is increased through practice and performance. In the discussion below, we illustrate not only the prevailing narratives and hierarchical structure of the FMO, but also the instrumental rewards offered in order to ensure and incentivize sanctioned practice. Though we separate and describe four distinct realms of the FMO—hierarchical structure, recruitment, prevailing narratives of whiteness, and instrumental incentives for practice—these distinct aspects of the FMO gain strength through recursive interaction. In this space of practice, which we see as the most structured and inescapable arm of whiteness within the mentoring program, there is less room for mentee agency than in the mentoring relationships described later in the chapter. First, we will use mentee descriptions to illustrate these four realms of the FMO and their interaction. Then, we will discuss opportunities, or lack of opportunities, for mentee agency that exist within the FMO.

### 4.1 Leadership and Hierarchy

It is clear in the interview transcripts that program staff Sam and Janet are highly visible to the mentees. Five of the nine mentees interviewed specifically mentioned these two members of the mentoring organization staff. Mentees assign specific hierarchical roles to each staff member and detail their past interactions. Sam Ford, a White man, is the director of the FMO and is seen by mentees both as a motivational figurehead and primary gatekeeper. Janet Baker, an African American woman, serves as the high school coordinator of the FMO, and is described by mentees as the main source of nurturing, playful interaction, and support within the program. Jasmine, a young African American woman in high school, stated: "Mrs. Baker (Janet) is an amazing woman. I just started working with her this year." Graduate of the program Kayli, another African American woman and current college student, also mentioned Janet, "You know, they've ... especially Sam and Janet, they've been great. You know, as far as everything, they help out; they're like the backbone especially when I was in high school." Statements about Janet reflect upon her warm and playful nature. Melissa, a Latina young woman says, "[Mrs. Baker is] really outgoing. She is funny. She just makes everything as a joke, which is fun." It is also apparent that mentees are very aware of the expectations that each staff member has for them, especially in the case of Sam. Melina stated:

> They help me with my grades when I go to them like Sam sometimes asks me if I have been doing good and I will be saying yes that I have been getting 3s, checks, and pluses. And he is like 'can you get pluses instead of checks' and I am like (laughs) 'yes.' And he has been like checking more to see how I have been doing. I like how Sam if you like, if he makes something really fun that you can learn and remember. I like how he makes it not boring; he makes it really fun and wow and awesome.

From Melina's statement, it seems that Sam functions in the program as a motivational voice. He specifically promotes academics and encourages participants to improve their grades. Additionally, mentees feel some responsibility to prove to Sam that they are academically successful and worthy of remaining in the program. As Melina mentions, Sam has the ability to "check in" on any of the participants. Interviewed mentees noted that these check-ins can deal with grades, teacher/student interactions, and even financial concerns. Valeria, another Latina young woman, spoke of his advice and how he checks in with her regarding academics.

> [The program] has been a great support. Especially Sam Ford. He has been one of those people who is always talking to you. He gives you all this advice that you can't help but to take into consideration. You can't just ignore it. Sam is one of those people you admire so much that you just want to impress all the time. He is one of the people that most likely whose advice you can take into consideration and just move on and say 'I can change this, I can improve this.' Especially with grades, he is always on you about grades. And that helps. It always nice to have one of those people who always care about, you know, you always having good grades and so, yeah, the rewards are really nice too.

Because FMO is a program of the local school district, the staff communicates directly with teachers regarding student grades, homework, and participation in class. In this way the staff, most notably Sam according to the students, practices a form of surveillance as a part of their role in the program. This surveillance allows them to be informed about student progress, but also enables the staff to make decisions about who can remain in the program and who cannot. In the following section, we will discuss mentee perceptions of access to and membership in the program.

### 4.2 Recruitment and Exclusivity

Throughout the program evaluation, our research group was particularly interested in how students become a part of the FMO. We learned that students are recommended in fourth grade, a process coordinated by their school social workers. Students are selected according to three criteria listed on the program website as: "Untapped potential that a mentor could help develop over time, [a student who is] actively seeking out adult attention, and a family who is willing to participate in the program." Though not listed as an official requirement, the website also notes that the program was founded specifically to "improve the achievement of African American and Latino students," thus adding the additional requirement that mentees be African American or Latino/a. The website also states, "Children are carefully selected for the program based on their ability to benefit from the increased support it offers. The neediest students are not necessarily chosen to participate."

When mentees speak about becoming a part of the program, some are unclear about how they became involved. Some credit a person, such as a parent, social worker, or teacher for signing them up for the program. Others, however, have detailed stories about seeking to join the program. Melina, a Latina young woman stated, "I became a part of it by my teacher and because I saw my sister and brother liking it a lot and how, like, they used to like learn a lot so I asked my mom if I could be in it and so we talked to my teacher and she said we could. Then we talked to Sam and he said we could cause I have really good report cards too." In this quote, Melina spoke about her impressions of the program. For example, as a young girl, she saw the program as something that her siblings enjoyed, and from which they "learned a lot." Again, it is important to note that Melina and her family see Sam as the gatekeeper who has the final say about acceptance into the program. Thus, even as we separate the distinct spaces of the FMO and mentoring relationships, we also acknowledge that membership to the FMO must be gained *prior* to being paired in a mentoring relationship. Whatever benefits are to be gained from the personal relationships with the mentor are filtered through each of the characteristics of the FMO described in this section.

Most important in the above quote from Melina is the statement "[Sam] said we could because I have really good grades." This loaded statement speaks not only about what is required to get into the program, but what might exclude someone from membership in the program. Though the program was

I DON'T THINK IT'S CHANGED ME, IT'S HELPED MOLD ME 99

founded with a mission to "increase achievement," in Melina's view students must have already attained a certain level of achievement for acceptance into the program. Alvaro, a young Latino man reinforces this belief, "[The FMO] has expectations, like if you don't have a 2.5 GPA, you don't ... you can't be in there. I've never been in a club before. So I mean, it was a good thing to get into." His statement also shows the influence of cultural imaginaries such as exclusivity and achievement, two social constructs often deeply implicated in the figured world of Whiteness, in this space. As the following statement from Melina shows, only students who meet the required GPA are deemed worthy of remaining in the program and can thus maintain access to a mentoring relationship. Melina stated, "I like how they changed the rules if you don't do good that they should get out of the program. You can't be in it unless you do good grades and improve because there are kids that actually do that." In this statement, Melina seems to be echoing the strong narrative of exclusivity put forth by the FMO. Indeed, her success and continued membership in the FMO may depend on adherence to such social constructs—imaginaries that we see as expectations for practice in a figured world of whiteness.

Aside from membership in the program, some of the mentees perceive their success in the program as a matter of how much Sam "likes" them. Valeria, a young Latina woman noted,

> It's always so exciting when you get your report card as a little kid and he would write notes on them and it would be like 'Yes! Sam likes me! Yes!' Or, you know, one note is like, 'Hey do you think you could have done better?" And it's like "Yessss." And it's just burn! Shame! I would tell him to keep that constructive criticism. It always helped students. It always helped me.

According to Valeria, Sam appreciating or liking a program participant is directly tied to how well they do on report cards and progress reports. In each of the mentee interviews, it was clear that grades and academics are central to mentees beliefs about the mission and work of the FMO. Within this framework, the FMO constructs a vision of self-worth that is directly tied to individual academic success. This represents a distinctly neoliberal narrative which excludes other possible narratives such as those that privilege collective or personal constructs of achievement.

### 4.3    *Sanctioned Imaginaries—Narratives of Whiteness*

As has been discussed above, a major message put forth by the FMO program is that of academic motivation and achievement. In order to maintain membership, students must improve and maintain their grades. In addition to this, there is significant emphasis on communication as a vehicle for achievement. Several mentees spoke about their experience in learning introduction, presentation, and organizational skills aimed at improving their professional communication. In speaking about a leadership institute program required of all participants, Valeria said,

> The [leadership institute camp] does all these sessions where they help you improve your speech and they help you improve your pauses and they just teach you all these things and you don't even realize it. You go back and you are like, "Hey I learned this in Leadership Institute or through FMO or Sam or whatever." [They have] lock-ins where you learn a lot about self-respect and self-image and having low self-esteem and how to improve it. And all these things that really help you later on ... you are just ready to go for it and you know you can do it because you had all these talks with people who gave you all this advice.

In this quote, Valeria describes events and workshops that aim to improve communication skills necessary for presentations. She identifies confidence and self-esteem as factors in successful presentation and achievement and states that practice and feedback during the workshops were helpful to her development. Notable in her statement is the implied assumption, by the FMO, that students are lacking in communication skills when they come to the program. In each of the interviews, students of all ages spoke strong statements of personal identity. As will be discussed in further detail below, we believe that this deficit assumption is incongruous to the strong personal agency that students report in their interviews. It also demonstrates how strongly whiteness is figured in this space of practice where dominant—whitestream—communication and linguistic practices are expected of mentees.

One specific example of communication skill used as a vehicle for achievement is the "First Place Introduction." Asked if he had any messages for Sam and the staff of the FMO, Rafael, a young Latino man stated:

> You should tell Sam that I did my First Place Introduction. He tries to get us to do it whenever we meet an adult. Whenever we have a workshop or an event, he always makes us do it and people kind of groan about it but I don't think it's kind of that bad. It's only like six [things] You say your name, grade, school you go to, what you want to be when you grow up, your strength. [Sam] said it opens up the door for us. He said that one time that this girl did it to someone and she said she wanted to be a trans-

lator and the person she told works at the hospital, I think, and he needed
someone to translate phone calls and he offered her a job.

Here, Rafael describes a script of communication for networking purposes. Again, this is communication aimed at increasing personal achievement, this time through active networking. This aspect of the FMO even comes with mythology, as Sam offered a specific story of an FMO graduate who benefitted from this introduction process. In this legend, achievement is defined as employment. Also of note is the fact that Rafael used the "First Place" introduction with the interviewer. This shows a certain level of trust and "buy-in" to the message that specific methods of communication are important, are valued, and lead to increased achievement. Kayli, an African American woman, echoed this positive perception of the communication skills that she learned through the program. She said, "[Sam and Janet] played a great role in my life. I think that the guidance [helped] my organization skills or my communication skills." As an adult, now in her early twenties, Kayli noted that she values these skills even more than she did as a participant in the program. She said that these skills have been instrumental, again, in helping her to gain employment.

### 4.4 Instrumental Rewards as Incentives for Practice
Throughout the interviews, mentees spoke plainly about the material goods and rewards that resulted from successful participation in the FMO. These goods exist outside of abstract constructs such as personal achievement, self-esteem, and satisfaction. To supplement the message of motivation put forth in a workshop entitled "Why Try?", mentees are offered trips and other experiences for making good or improved grades. Simone, an African American young woman spoke to the effectiveness of the reward model for her success,

> Like I know what motivated me a lot for getting good grades and studying was like, at the end of the quarter if you got A's and B's, they would take you bowling or ice skating or to Frankie's [a local games and amusement arcade]. And even now, even like right now, I'm in high school, but that all motivates me still. Like "Oh, why not?" The surprise at the end!

Rafael positions the instrumental rewards differently, qualifying them as *another* avenue for motivation. He said, "Well, I mean, they offer rewards for whenever you do good in school and so I think that is just another thing for, like another reason for me to do better." Earlier in his interview, Rafael had spoken passionately about the "Why Try?" workshop and the intrinsic motivation he felt from the messages learned there. In the above quote, he then spoke about instrumental rewards, or external motivation, as being in support of the overall mission of the FMO. Alex, an African American young man, sums up many of the mentees feelings on the methods of motivation used by the FMO, very clearly highlighting frequent rewards as appealing and motivating:

> [T]hey push you to [succeed], but they reward you when you do [succeed] ... achieve the goal that they want you to achieve. And so, it's kind of like a teacher almost, but with an award every day.

The majority of rewards that the students spoke of were trips or experiences that cost money for admission or attendance. Like many other institutions, the FMO has a capital exchange system in which students achieve "capital gains" by completing a task or a job. Most obviously, the requirements of the exclusive FMO membership involve sustained improvement and achievement in academics as adherence to sanctioned expectations. Outside of the short-term achievement goals and rewards detailed by Simone in which quarterly report card grades are rewarded with a bowling trip, students are also "rewarded" for their continued long-term membership in the program.

A major benefit of the program for most of the mentees and parents interviewed was the enrichment or activity funding, camp scholarships, and college scholarships offered by the program. Jasmine, an African American young woman, described the process of financial assistance provided through the FMO, "[T]hey can help you with so much. Like if [you need] something, they will be there with it. Like camp, the money for scholarships or anything like that, they will provide for you." Valeria also explained,

> And it's a nice thing to have the FMO to support us. And, especially financially you know because they do that. It just helps us with sports and certain stuff like that. I used my enrichment funding for my cheerleading and stuff because I have to pay for so much stuff. And it's just so expensive and they helped pay for that this year and last year. It's just been nice to have that support. As well as my brother and sister, they use it for soccer. And it's just really nice to have that.

Of the other mentees interviewed—including Kayli, Rafael, Alvaro, Melina, and Melissa—most mentioned the appeal of monetary rewards and funding as a component of the program. In fact, money was mentioned in interviews with parents and mentees more than any other singular topic. Shannon, Kayli's mom, even mentioned that the program provided her with Christmas funds one year when money was tight. Both parents and students are aware of the potential for the FMO to fund extracurricular experiences, school trips, and eventually post-secondary education. It also appears that parents and mentees take strategic advantage of the monetary rewards offered by the FMO. It is important to note here that mentees only continue to benefit from the program if they maintain an appropriate GPA, so this funding and membership can be taken away if a student is no longer meeting the academic requirements of the FMO. Thus, the instrumental rewards provided by the FMO are only provided through sustained and successful performance based on expectations set forth in the organization, expectations dictated by white-normed perspectives and assumptions.

## 4.5 *Strength of Message and Opportunities for Agency*

In summary, the space of practice associated with the FMO is one that, though highly structured, does allow for specific types of agency. However, this agency is highly constrained in that mentees may choose to adopt dominant narratives of achievement or they may reject these narratives, and thus choose to opt out. These two choices, the primary agentic choices available in this space of practice, are important to note. It is only through enthusiastic "buy-in" of FMO narratives that mentees gain access to the space of mentoring relationships where there are more opportunities for agency. As Valeria stated, "You can't just ignore [Sam's advice]." Her statement represents the strong implications of whiteness and the inescapable character of the FMO. The space of practice discussed in this section is one where the potency of whiteness has great strength. Again, a figured world gains strength through practice and performance (Holland, 2012). In this case, the FMO is strategically constructed such that mentees must practice according to expectation, or else be excluded. The instrumental rewards offered by the FMO, including significant monetary funding, function as incentives encouraging sanctioned performance. However, while we note significant constraints within the FMO, we see more opportunity for mentee agency in the space of individual mentoring relationships.

## 5 Second Space of Practice: Mentoring Relationships

The relationship of students to the FMO was characterized by defined boundaries, specific expectations, succinct messaging, and various instrumentalities or exchanges. When we coded and analyzed the student's interview texts in regards to their relationship with their mentors, many of the descriptive themes changed substantively. Certainly the topics of interaction often overlapped with discussions from the previous section about favored leaders, goals, accomplishments, program events, and rewards for meeting expectations or goals. But, nevertheless, the highly instrumental space of the FMO (that constantly invokes the many of the markers and symbols of the figured world of whiteness) with its common goals and boundaries yielded to a more intimate and often more agentic space when the conversation was redirected to specific mentoring relationships. Even the messaging about goals and accomplishments were situated in personal relationship. In this discourse of greater relationality in this realm, one begins to see some of the agency that was rarely present in the FMO as a space of practice.

## 5.1    *Friendship*
As we studied the transcripts of these interviews, the language of friendship was prominently used by students in reference to their relationship with their mentors. The process of inclusion in the mentoring organization and the common messaging about academic success may have framed the expectations of the students as they began their mentoring relationships, but the students seemed to quickly find that their relationship with their mentors would go far beyond these expectations. Valeria expressed this transformation of expectation and experience:

> When I first joined it, I was just expecting a mentor like a school tutor in some sort of way. But it was completely different from what I expected. I guess the fact that the mentors are actually, they actually hang out with you as part of the family. And they would take you out to eat and the movies. And we would go sometimes swimming and all these different I guess adventures that I had never done before. It was just things I had never done before and it was just nice to get out there and do all these new things that I guess living here and Latina I was not exposed to.

As Valeria continued describing her relationship with her mentor, the enthusiasms of friendships such as an emotional bond, commitment, sustained time together, encouragements, and life sharing as well as the normal friendship challenges such as emotional and logistical struggles were clearly marked in this relationship.

> I mean we have had little hard patches here and there but overall nothing has ever separated us. There was a point where I guess she started working a lot so we didn't see each other as much, but we would make time for each other eventually. You know it would be like every time we saw each other, it would be much more exciting because it would be like 'oh

I DON'T THINK IT'S CHANGED ME, IT'S HELPED MOLD ME 105

my god I have so much to tell you.' And, oohh, and first this and first that we would plan to meet for like three hours and then time would fly by and we would end up spending seven hours at her house just watching a movie or me helping her cook or we would go out. And she was actually the person who got me to swim at a pond. Never done that before. It was rough but I got through. She is that person for me. I could always look for and say this whenever I am upset and I know she is always there for me.

Alex, testified to the strength of his relational bond with his mentor, "Me and my mentor, we're like best friends. He includes me in almost a lot of the places that he goes, unless it's like business-wise ... but yeah, it's really close." Kayli described the relational nature of her mentoring relationship as follows:

I remember we would go to museums, college tours. Sometimes we would meet up with other mentors and their mentees and do stuff with them. Go out to eat, go to the movies. Sometimes we would just hang around. I remember we planted a garden one time, and we cooked from a recipe and stuff like that.

She then summarized her description of the relationship with a statement of ongoing interaction and friendship, "Oh yeah, I still talk to her. Sarah's awesome, I love Sarah." Rafael echoed these same sentiments as he described his relationship with his mentor:

Well we talk a lot ... I think we are really good friends. Usually, we always go out to eat before or after what we do and that always gives us time to talk and catch up on what's happening in our lives. So, I think we are very close.

Reflecting on these interviews, these students not only freely used the language of friendship to label their relationships with individual mentors, when describing these relationships in greater detail, they crafted narratives of loyalty, affection, fun, encouragement, and even occasional squabbles that are easily recognized as the earmarks of ongoing friendships.

## 5.2 Familial Affirmations

In many cases these descriptions of relational intimacy with their mentors were accompanied by, replaced with, or intensified by familial affirmations in regards to the relational status of their mentors with the students and often the students' extended families. Valeria very adeptly described a relationship with her mentor that began formally and then the formality yielded to friendship:

At first it was like, 'oh she is an adult' and you have to have that respect for her and whenever she would ask me something it would just be like, 'yes, yes, sure of course.' It was really polite but then it just got to a point where it was just chill and she was my best friend. She is really young. Well, when I met her, she was really young and she still is in my radar even though she doesn't think so. And we just get along so well because I guess our personalities are really similar. We are both really outgoing and when we are around each other, we are just like really silly and goofy and we play around with each other a lot. I got to a point where I just felt really comfortable sharing anything with her.

Within the same narrative, Valeria also intermingled direct and even formal family affirmations about her mentor:

I feel like my relationship now for me, we are kind of like sisters ... And I guess that's ... it's really nice to have that, because to me it's not like she is just a role model, she is practically family. Especially with our families, she considers herself "la gringa de la familia" (the white girl of the family) and, umm, it's just so nice. I love having her around. She is my godmother actually, for my communion. So yes, she is very close to the family. She is family. That's what we tell her.

Melissa described her mentor in similar familial language and also mentioned a similar connection of her mentor to the extended family: "She's like my sister to me and ... I mean, I can tell her everything and she helps me out with everything and she's like always there for my family too." Speaking of her mentor, Jasmine declared, "I call her my aunt and my mom."

Certainly some of the relationships that have taken on the characteristics of deep friendship or family between mentors and mentees are enhanced by the youthfulness of the mentors and, on occasion, shared ethnicity. Valeria spoke of the young age of her mentor, "We are kind of like sisters. She is really young. Well, when I met her, she was really young." Melissa explained her first mentoring relationship with a White mentor was more difficult:

Okay. So with a White one, it was kind of hard. Like she understood a little bit of Spanish. So ... like I'm ... when I speak English, I sometimes put a lot of Spanish into it. I do that a lot. So with her, I couldn't do that. I'm like I had to stop myself a lot. Um, and for example, you know how some Latino people do things because of their culture, things like that, and then they do their stuff different 'cause of their culture. So our culture would be different and I'd be like, "Why is she doing that?"

When her first mentor moved away, Melissa was connected with a Latina mentor and this relationship was considerably easier for her:

But with Yareli, I mean, yes, she is from a different place, but she's still Latino, right. I mean, it's like the same thing. We connect easily. We talk Spanish and English. Um, yeah, she understands and I understand her a lot.

Nevertheless, most of these relationships transcended their differences of age, ethnicity, and social context to the point that it became natural to speak of the relationship in terms of deep friendship or familial connection. Previously, we noted that Valeria's mentor considered herself to be "la gringa de la familia," a claim that seemed to be well received by Valeria and her whole family. Valeria specifically explained how she and her mentor had bridged potential racial boundaries through the shared racial values and the development of mutual respect:

Even though she is white and I am Mexican, she has a lot of respect for other races ... She likes diversity just like I do. And mostly because it's not like she likes specific groups of people like only Mexicans or African Americans. No she likes all kinds of races. And she believes a lot in other races. She believes that every student, no matter where they come from, or how old he or she is, always has some creativity and some intellectual smartness ... I have respect for her race. And, I guess, even though ... the media always shows this white dominant figure as the ideal figure or vice versa with men or women, apart from that I just admire her for the person she is.

Jasmine also testified how she and her mentor transcended both racial and age differences:

Well my mentor, she's like my ... I call her aunt and my mom. Um, she's very nice. She's white She's an older woman. She works at the art museum. But yeah, basically ... she looks at me like ... like a little niece from a different race, um, and we just like connect so much and we've been through a lot together.

The cases of Jasmine and Valeria differ somewhat than Melissa's experience. In each case, the space of mentoring has been a context where they have constructed an intimate, familial relationship despite some significant differences.

### 5.3 *Instrumentalities, Personal Relationships, and Agency*

Some of the contrasts between the space of the FMO and that of personal mentoring relationships are now quite evident. In the previous section, we looked closely at the leadership of the organization, specific boundaries of memberships, its prevailing messages of achievement and image, and the role of material goods or instrumental rewards for students who followed the plan. Exchange, reward, goal-setting, and achievement are all highly valued within this organizational context, constantly invoking the dominant paradigm of whiteness. Many of these instrumentalities were naturally present in the relationships with personal mentors as reported by the students. This is certainly to be expected since students were selected because they demonstrated the characteristics of and desire for potential success, and therefore they were likely to take advantage of the opportunities presented by the FMO. Nonetheless, these instrumentalities were often deeply enmeshed with and defined by a personal relationship within the mentoring context. These students often spoken of being urged, challenged, and even pushed. But these subtle and not so subtle nudges toward life's possibilities and rewards, some clearly evoked from a rationale of whiteness, were often received within the relational contexts of friendship, respect, trust, and admiration. In other words, the figuring and construction of ambition, rewards, and expectations occurred in the highly personal context of mentoring. Within this relationality, one begins to see growing evidence of agency among the mentees. Melissa spoke in several instances about her mentor's strong urgings and suggestions related to Melissa's growth:

> She pushes me to ... to do something better, 'cause she knows that I'm that type of person that I want to go to college to show people that just because you're Latino doesn't mean you can't go to college. And she's like, "If you want to do this, you have ... you have to go to Writing Camp," for example, or things like that, and my mom does that too.

In this instance, she connected her mentor's expectations to those of her parents and hence warmly received those nudges as an impetus to challenge herself with new experiences. Yet, some of these opportunities or challenges were met with resistance. Melissa continued:

> She takes me to do a lot of volunteer work 'cause I usually don't do things like that. So, she takes me to do a lot of volunteer work; makes me try something new all the time, even though I don't like to.

In both circumstances, attending writing camp or the volunteer work that she doesn't like, Melissa justifies her acquiescence in terms of her personal relationship with mentor. Referring to writing camp, Melissa affirmed the importance of her mentor's life story, "Since [she's] Latina, she knows what I'm going through right now, so she like puts her stories as an example." These life stories have clearly had a strong impact on Melissa:

> Like ... hmm. She told me a story one day like about her parents. They weren't able to go to college ... she just tells me how ... how a lot of other people thought that she wouldn't be able to go to college because she's Latina and how she got to show people that she is still at college. She can, like, do what she wants; it doesn't matter if you're Black, White, Latino. You can do whatever you want no matter where you come from.

Regarding that volunteer work and summarizing this relationship, Melissa added, "You know, she just motivates me to do something new all the time."

Kayli also described a relationship of nudging and gentle urgings by her mentors as well as some resistance similar to that of Melissa's:

> She is always giving me her point of view. I mean, I might not want to hear it, but you know, it always like, works best. And sometimes I get advice from her—I don't exactly listen to it at first and then it like dawns on me, "This is what [she] was saying!" She stays on top of me. Even for, like applying for university now, she's like "Kayli, make sure you do this, and make sure you do that."

Kayli's recognition of her mentor's wisdom and justification of her receptivity to her mentor's advice is deeply rooted in the admiration and respect that Kayli has for her. In this case, relationship supersedes Kayli's high goals and desires for success as a motivation:

> I love [her] I still keep in contact with [her]. Umm, I guess, just seeing [her] and how she's accomplished, how she speaks to her goals. [She] inspires me, honestly And [she] has always been like a great support system as far as like, encouraging me and she tells me, like, I can come to her and talk to [her] about anything.

Kayli and Melissa both testified to a persistence of nudging, urging, suggestion making, and goal setting coming from mentors to mentees. But this norm of nudges and even insistence on occasion from mentors does not preclude agency from mentees. Melissa humorously displayed her intractability to her mentor's stated goal that she read a book over the summer:

Well, see, the truth is, I don't read at home or nothing. I'm like that type of person that I have to read at school because I have to; I have no choice. But if you give me a book to read in the summer, I'm not gonna read it!

Throughout our analysis, we found both active and passive acts of resistance to mentoring among the interviewed students. This could take the form of the rejection of advice from mentors, resistance to guidance that may or may not have ultimately changed after longer reflection or greater experience, or the passive resistance of simply meeting less often with unfavorable mentors.

In many cases, the relationalities of mentoring and the agency associated with relationship trumped the instrumentalities of exchange often present within the mentoring context or contended with some of the active recruitment of whiteness. Jasmine's description of her relationship with her mentor offered a strong example of how various instrumentalities of personal goals and rewards are defined by or are secondary to relationship. In her recounting, these instrumentalities, as we have called them, were strong motivations in the formation of her relationship with her mentor:

My mom really likes [her]. She really thinks that she is really, like, a good person and my mom always says like I need to like stay nice to her, I need to respect her, and I need to like ... 'cause she will give me opportunities that my mom couldn't. Like I really need to stick with her and I need to like never slack off with her 'cause she's done so much for me.

This certainly may have been the situation with some of the other students. There is little doubt that organizational aims the FMO, including its common messaging as well as the strong its insistent expectations of goal setting and seeking success by selected students, had a powerful impact in framing these mentoring relationships. Recall Valeria's previously reported expectation, "When I first joined it, I was just expecting a mentor like a school tutor in some sort of way." Nevertheless, relationships in the context of mentoring, typically described as close friendships or family relations, have had a transformative impact on the experience of the students such that goals and hopes of these students became deeply connected to those relationships. Though Jasmine may have begun her relationship with her mentor with a goals and rewards mindset, she reported a very similar tone and progression of her mentoring relationship to that of Melissa and Kayli's experiences:

> If she sees that I'm failing ... she like gets on me. "You need to do this." And
> she just ... like she stays on top of me, and, yeah, we have ... sometimes
> [we] yell at each other; we fuss and scream. But then again, we love each
> other and we like ... we really do have a [strong] relationship. And some-
> times I feel like, "Just shut up," because she just gets on my nerves. Then
> like the next like hour I will give her a hug and a kiss.

Once again, the report includes a relationship with urgings and insistences that
include moments of resistance and frustration. But above all, the mentoring
relationship is marked by care, friendship, and students expressing agency that
is consistent with the norms of relationship. They feel free to fight, make-up,
ignore advice, disdain simple goals (like Melissa's unwillingness to read over
the summer!), and change their mind related to the nudging and urgings from
their mentors.

Jada's reflection on the importance of mentoring in her life affirms not
only the importance of relationality in this context, but also reveals a common act of agency among the interviewed students—to resist the suggestions
of their mentors and then later to embrace that advice after greater personal
experience:

> When I first got my mentor, I was in seventh grade, like I said, and that ...
> *she changed my life*. Like she was the best mentor. Then I got another one
> and they just helped me progress with my future. And then, like now, I
> look back and they gave me the greatest advice that I probably didn't take
> then, but I'm gonna take it now. (emphasis added)

Jada exhibits, like many of these students, agency in relationship. In our first
space of practice, that of the FMO, our data revealed constant evidence of
instrumental relationships, wherein motivated students fulfilled the expectations of the FMO through the development and support of goals generated in
the values of often the FMO. This is a contextual relationship dominated by
the notion of boundary, expectation, exchange, and reward. The shift to this
second space of practice is significant. The mentoring space was constantly
characterized by descriptions of friendship and familial relationship. Even in
places where the calculations of exchange were present, the relational context
often defined these encounters deeply. Also, significantly present were earmarks of student agency consistent with the expectations of give-and-take in
relationship. As we move to a final data section, that of assertions and affirmations in both spaces of practice, one sees even greater marks of student agency.

## 6 Assertions and Descriptions: The Marks of Self-Authoring and Student Agency

The student interviews in this project exhibited a remarkable amount of 'I plan to' assertions about personal goals and 'I am' statements of personal description. The sheer volume of these types of statements was one of the first observations we made in beginning to code this data. Career goals constantly appeared in the dialogue of these students in discussing their relationships with the FMO and their mentors. They were equally quick to describe their strengths and weaknesses. Perhaps very consistent to their training in conveying a First Place introduction, the students spoke freely and confidently, often about goals and personal characteristics. Melissa serves as an excellent example. She described first her progression to aspiring to become a dentist thusly:

> Like ever since I got my braces, I got to like ... I want[ed] to be a dentist. At first I wanted to be a lawyer, to help immigration people. But then I decided I wanted to be a dentist. Then she immediately described her strengths. I think people see in me how nice I am, friendly, funny supposedly, and like how outgoing I am and how I try really hard to like to get to what I want to ... I'm good at making people when they're upset or like when they're having a bad day [feel better]. Yeah, I'm good at math and track.

Shannon spoke of a growing maturity and focus after initial stubbornness and lack of focus on academics. Valeria described her love of learning, a passion for working with kids, and an ultimate goal being a pediatrician. Rafael expressed his desire to be architect or engineer and his skills as a soccer player. He confidently affirmed his relational and academic strengths:

> Most of my friends see me as like a friend that they can trust and someone they can hang out with. My teachers, well I think they see me as being smart with a good future.

Melina told us she was apt in art and math and was known as a risk taker who even tried things she despite not being sure she would be skillful or successful. Jasmine touted her communication skills and ambition being "the type of girl that actually wants to do something with her life." Simone, with a wink and a nod, accepted her reputation as "the Hispanic nerd at [her] school." She continued by comfortably offering explanations of how she was conservative (not "wild and crazy"), yet also very sociable. Tiana told us about her love for chorus, dance, and as she said, "you know I can talk!" At every pass through the interview data, we were drawn not only to the volume of these assertions and descriptions, but also to the confidence, self-awareness, and determination that often accompanied them. We were not sure what to make of these statements. But they "felt" agentic to us and we kept coming back to them in our analysis.

Demonstrating both her skill of articulation and her obvious passion for life, Tiana was one of several mentees who helped us with this dilemma. Tiana was asked serendipitously if she felt "in control" of her many expressed goals. To this she affirmed—

> All of them. I'm in control of all of 'em. Just like … just like your mother birthed you, but from that point all she can do is just push you out of the nest. "Come on, you got it." That's all she can do. She can't really tell you to turn left when you need to turn right … You have to know what you need to do.

In this determination, Tiana was not ignoring the many constraints in her life nor the agency of others including the urgings and expectations of teachers and mentors. Responding to a question about her African American heritage, she acknowledged, "Oh, we came from slavery." But, considering the support of family, several mentors, and a significant ISS (in school suspension) teacher who challenged her to reflect on her life during a season when she was a "troublemaker," she rejoiced, "Everybody, literally everybody in my life has been pushing me forward." But to the enduring struggle of race and its powerful wake in present lives, Tiana rebuked the idea that these horrific events would dominate "my education or my future—because it's my future. I have the choice. It … it's my choice whether I want to go further or if I want to be a bum on the street." Thankful of the support she has received, Tiana boldly opined:

> We, yeah, we can go anywhere we want to go and don't let nobody and don't let anything think that you can't. And sometimes it is because of your hard background, which makes you want to like climb up that, the steepest mountain. It's like I want to go to the top because I've been at the bottom and I know what it's like.

We remain fully aware of the lasting impediments due to the enduring struggles that she mentions as well as the structural confinements as well as encouragement originating in the expectations of the FMO, the urgings of mentors, and the powerful recruitments of the figured world of whiteness that we have described in earlier sections of this chapter. Nonetheless, we could not ignore the strong perception of agency among these students and the growing sense in our analysis that agency remained despite these constraints.

## 7 Mentoring and Everyday Agency

Holland et al. (2008) make a very useful distinction about agency that offers greater understanding regarding of Tiana's and so many other of the mentees' assertions of unlimited futures and declarations of personal capability. They define agency as "the socioculturally mediated capacity of an actor to make a difference, to have effects *in,* if not *on,* a social world" (Holland et al., 2008). This possibility of agency *in,* if not *on,* social worlds is quite significant, allowing for a distinction between *everyday agency* and *transformative agency* (agency that changes the world). They define everyday agency as "the basic sort of agency afforded to humans by language, and by extension, culture. Language clearly provides communicative resources for representing and enacting past, present, and future realities" (Holland et al., 2008). They drew on the work of linguistic anthropologist, Alessandro Duranti, who explained further, "Any act of speaking involves some kind of agency ... by speaking we establish a reality that has at least the potential for affecting whoever happens to be listening to us" (Duranti, 2004). Following this work, we assert that the declarations and personal descriptions of these students are marks of at least an everyday agency that remains and thrives despite the legacies of enduring struggles, the power of racial figured worlds, and the firm structures of well-intended organizations such as the FMO in a whitestream world. These students form intimate identities in all these contexts and agency is derived from these identities.

Agency, through being addressed in our social worlds and our responses in these same social worlds, has been theorized in the works of George Herbert Mead and Mikhail Bakhtin. Mead's work described intricately how personal or intimate identities are fashioned in the social through his introduction of an "I-me" system. In this work, the 'me' is a person's reply to both his own talk and that of social interaction. The 'I' does not exist as an object of full consciousness (it is not fully known), but the conversational nature of our inner lives does indeed imply an 'I' behind our consciousness (Mead, 1912). The intimate self, the "I," is deeply impacted by groups and community (Mead, 1913). "This self becomes as object, an other unto himself, through the very fact that he hears himself talk and replies" (Mead, 1912, p. 377). Mead (1912) explained, "Inner consciousness is socially organized by the importation of the social organization of the outer world."

Bakhtin's (1981) work on self-authoring is a crucial addition to the dynamics of intimate identities formed in local spaces of practice or the 'social' in Mead's premise. His ideas on *dialogism* and the *space of authoring* rescue, for many, the notion of human agency against many totalitarian or deterministic views of culture. Dialogism is a way to explain that humans in figured worlds exist perpetually in a reality of being addressed and answering. The meaning constructed by answering the varying voices, or vocal perspectives of culture, becomes an act of authoring the self. "In answering, the self 'authors' the world—including itself and others" (Holland et al., 1998, p. 173). In effect, the world is seen or perceived in the dialogic practice of authoring. Over time, internally persuasive discourses develop to mediate these conflicting voices in a movement toward the creation of a relatively stable authorial stance.

The explication of dialogism is a strong reminder of the ever becoming and forming nature of identity. Lachicotte (2002) demonstrated the space of authoring to truly be a field of contestation. In the space of authoring, "none of us is occupied singularly; we are not possessed by one identity, one discourse, one subject-position" (Lachicotte, 2002, p. 61). Lachicotte (2002) described this sourcing of agency quite eloquently, "Yet, selves remain powers in return: as we answer to the world's manifold address, so it must answer to ours" (p. 62).

The students in our study are constantly being addressed by a legacy of enduring struggles, the expectations of mentors, a FMO that expects that they will progress in their accomplishments, and a resilient figured world of whiteness that often defines the nature of success and progress. But, in these remarkable assertions and statements of self-description, we see these students answering and self-authoring in the midst of these structures and relationships. Their agency is often that of everyday agency as compared to transformative agency. They do not often proclaim the power to change the world they are thrust into. The students in the study often fluctuated between hyper-awareness of the struggles of the world they live in and nonchalance about the impediments of race and social class. The figured world of whiteness was often evoked in their lives, true to its nature invisible normal that permeates life and maintains power in its deniability. Nonetheless, their speech does reveal an agency that is not to be dismissed. As their identities have been impacted in the social worlds of a FMO and the high relational context of mentoring, they impact themselves and others in their speech and expectations forged in concert with these social worlds.

## 8    Summary

In this chapter, we have described two specific spaces of practice within the studied FMO. Using participant descriptions, we elaborated the space of this FMO as a location heavily subsumed by a figured world of whiteness. Practice in this white-normed space is driven by achievement-based narratives of success, accountability, and motivation. Expectations for participation and practice in this space are highly structured and seemingly inescapable, leaving very little room for mentee agency. Indeed, the FMO grants monetary reward for appropriate performance and adherence to its organizational narratives. We allow for the possibility that some families are well aware of the overarching narrative of whiteness, but choose to use the program so that their children may have access to funding for extracurricular activities and experiences. Students-of-color are constantly navigating white-normed spaces of practice, and may find themselves willing and able to "play the game" as Urrieta (2009) stated—working from within a figured world.

The second space of practice, mentoring relationships, is an area where the participants alluded to more opportunity for personal agency. In the relational contexts of friendship, respect, trust, and mutual admiration, we saw mentees both accepting and resisting guidance from their mentors. Mentees described significant moments in their relationship with a mentor when they questioned the mentor's advice or even refused to engage. In these moments, students exercise a type of *everyday agency* that effectually changes or influences the mentoring relationship. We do not go as far as to say that this type of agency represents *transformative agency* as described by Holland et al. (2008). Mentoring relationships only take place when students successfully ascribe to narratives set forth by the FMO, which we have described as situated firmly in a figured world of whiteness.

Finally, we felt compelled to note mentee assertions of identity and agency that appeared so prominently in interview data. We see these statements as being directly related to our argument that everyday agency persists, despite the ever-looming horizon of whiteness and its dominant expectations. Mentees maintain a complex vision of their relational and aspirational worlds. Though influenced by the FMO, this vision is also constructed through interaction with peers, teachers, and family. As Kayli stated, she sees that the program has helped to "mold her," but it hasn't changed who she is at the core of her intimately constructed self. In conclusion, we note significant marks of everyday agency enacted by mentees in the organization, despite the overwhelming presence of a figured world of whiteness.

### References

Bakhtin, M. M. (1981). *The dialogic imagination: Four essays* (M. E. Holquist, Ed., C. Emerson & M. Holquist, Trans.). Austin, TX: University of Texas Press.

Bettez, S. C. (2011). Navigating the guilt vs. innocence dichotomy in teaching social justice. *South Atlantic Philosophy of Education Society 2011 Yearbook*, 169–181.

Burawoy, M. (1998). The extended case method. *Sociological Theory, 16*(1), 4–33.

Duranti, A. (2004). Agency in Language. In A. Duranti (Ed.), *A companion to linguistic anthropology* (pp. 451–473). Malden, MA: Blackwell.

Hatt, B. (2011). Smartness as a cultural practice in schools. *American Educational Research Journal, 20*(10), 1–23.

Holland, D. (2012). Oral description in a seminar on November 30, 2012.

Holland, D., Lachicotte, W., Skinner, D., & Cain, C. (1998). *Identity and agency in cultural worlds.* Cambridge, MA: Harvard University Press.

Holland, D., Lachicotte Jr., W., Skinner, D., & Cain, C. (2008). Positional identities. In P. Murphy & K. Hall (Eds.), *Learning and practice: Agency and identities* (pp. 149–160). Thousand Oaks, CA: Sage Publications.

Holland, D., & Lave, J. (2001). History in person: An introduction. In D. Holland & J. Lave (Eds.), *History in person: Enduring struggles, contentious practice, intimate identities* (pp. 3–33). Albuquerque, NM: School of American Research Press.

Hytten, K., & Warren, J. (2003). Engaging whiteness: How racial power gets reified in education. *Qualitative Studies in Education, 16*(1), 65–89.

Lachicotte, W. (2002). Intimate powers, public selves: Bakhtin's space of authoring. In J. Mageo (Ed.), *Power and the self* (pp. 48–66). New York, NY: Cambridge University Press.

Marx, S. (2004). Regarding whiteness: Exploring and intervening in the effects of White racism in teacher education. *Equity and Excellence in Education, 37*(1), 31–43.

Mead, G. H. (1912). The mechanism of social consciousness. *Journal of Philosophy, Psychology, and Scientific Methods, 9*(15), 401–406.

Mead, G. H. (1913). The social self. *Journal of Philosophy, Psychology, and Scientific Methods, 10*(14), 374–380.

Tavory, I., & Timmermans, S. (2009). Two cases of ethnography: Grounded theory and the extended case method. *Ethnography, 10*(3), 243–263.

Urrieta, L. (2009). *Working from within: Chicana and Chicano activist educators in whitestream schools.* Tucson, AZ: University of Arizona Press.

Valenzuela, A. (1999). S*ubtractive schooling: U.S.- Mexican youth and the politics of caring*. Albany, NY: SUNY Press.

Warren, J. T. (2001). Doing whiteness: On the performative dimensions of race in the classroom. *Communication Education, 50*(2), 91–108.

CHAPTER 5

# Inculcando *Confianza:* Towards Exploring the Possibilities in the Mentoring of Latina Youth

*Esmeralda Rodriguez*

## 1     Introduction

Latina youth often find themselves having to straddle two worlds: the world of the home—where they must exemplify respect and honor family obligations and the "Anglo" world (Salguero & McCusker, 1996)—which stresses the importance of individualism. While engaging in this cultural straddling, they must also contend with how to respond to low expectations from others in order to pursue their goals (Denner & Guzman, 2006). Schools have used mentoring programs to address the inequalities and "social challenges" faced by *at risk* girls (Quarles, Maldonado, & Lacey, 2005, p. 2).

However, it is important to recognize that mentoring is not a neutral act. Both the mentor and the mentee are operating within the same systems that have (re)produced the inequalities they seek address. Without critically engaging the mentoring relationship and its purpose, programs aimed at correcting deficits and maintaining status quos can result in subtractive rather than additive experiences. For students of color, this results in the reinforcement of hegemonic, white, middle class conventions of social and cultural capital. Mentoring relationships need to not only address the mentee's "diversity status" but also their "social identities" and be responsive to their racial and ethnic identities, families, socio-economic statuses, religion, etc. from a critical and non-deficit perspective (Liang & Grossman, 2010, p. 239).

This chapter strives, in part, to address issues of power between the mentor, mentee, and mentee's family. I argue that in addition to mentors and mentees acting as partners, the mentor must also establish a partnership with the mentee's family. In the mentoring program described in this book, students of color are overwhelmingly paired with white mentors, thus, begging the question of *who can and should* mentor youth of color. Another question that begs to be addressed is: who can a mentor look towards to inform their mentoring practices? In this chapter, I wish to disrupt who can be a source of knowledge and inspiration in the mentorship of Latina youth. I seek to unpack of the cultural concept of *confianza* from the perspective of two Latina mothers living

© KONINKLIJKE BRILL NV, LEIDEN, 2019 | DOI: 10.1163/9789004407985_006

in North Carolina, and explore the implications and possibilities for the mentorship of Latina youth.

## 2　Why Latina Mothers Matter in the Mentorship of Their Daughters

I draw from Chicana feminist scholars to inform my theoretical and epistemological grounding. Chicana feminist scholars seek to dismantle the historically deficit and peripheral frames that compound the systems of oppression that Chicanas are subject to (Delgado Bernal, 1998). Chicana feminist theory centers lived experiences and Chicana feminist scholars "theorize … lived experience as a knowledge base to understand, critique, and challenge system oppression and theorize identity, sexuality, the body, resistance, healing, transformation, and empowerment" (Pérez Huber & Cueva, 2012, p. 395). One way Chicana scholars have done this is by redefining everyday experiences and culturally specific ways of teaching and knowing as important sources of knowledge—particularly, communal knowing (Delgado Bernal, 2002; Villenas, Godinez, Delgado Bernal, & Elenes, 2006). Chicana feminist scholarship has elucidated multiple ways of teaching and knowing amongst Chicanas. They are, to name a few, the concept of *educación, la facultad* (knowing through experience and intuition), *consejos* (narrative advice), *respeto* (respect), and *valerse por si misma* (self reliance) (Villenas et al., 2006; Elenes, Gonzalez, Delgado Bernal, & Villenas, 2001; Valdes, 1996). Chicana feminist theory is a theory of agency that is woman centered and woman defined. Chicana feminist scholarship frames mothers as central figures to their children's socialization and serve as the conduits through which cultural knowledge is transmitted (Villenas et al., 2006).

Mothers can serve as an inspiration of resiliency and teach young Latinas to advocate for themselves and persevere. For example, in Carrillo and Rodríguez (2016), María revealed that her motivation to succeed academically was driven by a desire to honor her mother's sacrifices as well as to help her *salir adelante.* According to DeLeon (1996), Latino families highly influence their children's decision making in regards to education, personal development and career aspirations. Latina/o cultures highly value familism—the strong identification with the nuclear/extended family exemplified by a strong sense of loyalty, mutual respect, support, and solidarity (Valdes, 1996). Because of the importance of collectivism, individual successes are considered family successes (DeLeon, 1996).

In their study on middle school Latinas, Lopez and Lechuga (2007) found that these students were able to resist the deficit frames that position them as underachieving, culturally flawed individuals (McLean Taylor, Veloria, & Verba, 2007) by seeking safe, nurturing spaces and companionship from other Latinas. The students specifically cited their Latina mothers (both their own and 'other-mothers') as confidants and teachers of resiliency. The women in these culturally empowering spaces provided a sense of authentic caring (Valenzuela, 1999) that inspired positive transformations of identity.

In his work on parent relationships with schools, Stanton-Salazár (2001) found that *confianza* was key to developing strong relationships. When there is *confianza* between people, there is an obligation that is constantly established and reinforced (Gonzalez et al., 1995). Stanton-Salazár and Urso Spina (2003) argued that Mexican immigrants have a "communitarian" orientation that is characterized by *confianza en confianza* (trust in trust). *Confianza en confianza* is learned through intimate and often family based social interactions or close peer interactions (Ream, 2005). In communitarian-oriented communities, there is a "psychocultural" expectation for ongoing and reciprocal generosity in trusting and intimate relations (Stanton-Salazár & Urso Spina, 2003). In my review of the literature, I have found that while *confianza* is a recurring and important cultural concept in Latina/o scholarship, there is a dearth of qualitative studies that address how *confianza* is taught, learned, reaffirmed, and used by Latina mothers. Further, there is a lack of research on what *confianza* may suggest for youth mentoring relationships. In this chapter, I seek to address those holes in the literature by looking towards how Latina mothers living in the New Latino south define and operationalize *confianza* in their families and communities. I also explore what can mentors learn from these mothers about establishing meaningful relationships with their mentees.

## 3    Latina Pedagogies in the New South

As the number of Latina/os increases in non-traditional Latina/o immigration states (Hamann, Worthham, & Murillo, 2002), Latina/os living in the New Latino Diaspora face unique challenges as "creators and forgers of new Latino communities" (Villenas, 2002, p. 30). Historically, Latinos have been absent from the demographic, economic, cultural, and political systems of the south, thus the increased Latino migration of the 1990's has caused a profound shift (Furuseth & Smith, 2006). This migration disrupted "the social status, economic relations, and public consciousness" (Furuseth & Smith, 2006, p. 2) long established by the Black and White racial dichotomy that dominates the south (Hamman & Harklau, 2010). Thus, Latina/os now face important questions about identity, race, and place in their new communities.

INCULCANDO CONFIANZA                                                      121

Hamann, Wortham, and Murillo (2002) argue that once Latina/os enter these new diaspora spaces, their "funds of knowledge" (Moll et al., 1992) can often be at odds with the racially dichotomous systems that exist in states like North Carolina, where this study takes place. In the creation of these new Latina/o communities, Latina/os are in a liminal state where they can either imagine themselves as part of these new communities or they can feel isolated and detached from them (Hamann, Worthham, & Murillo, 2002); they must also contend with being simultaneously framed as an asset and a problem by those in power (Furuseth & Smith, 2006).

Scholarship on the New Latino Diaspora has found that public institutions such as schooling have not been responsive to new communities of Latina/o parents and their children (Hamann, Worthham, & Murillo, 2002) and often, Latina/os have been reduced to their worker status and seen as a problem that needs to be fixed (Villenas, 2001; Murillo, 2002). Latina/os have been framed as a needy group of people whose differences in race, language, and class rendered them culturally flawed. There emerged programs that, at face value, offered assistance to Latina/os. However, Latina/os were at the risk of being reduced their plight and thus being seen as clients, rather than people with agency (Villenas, 2001). For example, Villenas (2001) described a program in Hope City, North Carolina that was designed to teach Latina mothers on how to be good parents. This program serves as an example of how benevolent racism (Villenas, 2001) can contribute to the historical and significant deficit rhetoric and public stigma surrounding Latina/os.

In her ethnographic study on the rural town, Hope City, North Carolina (Villenas, 2001; Villenas & Moreno, 2001; Villenas, 2002; Villenas, 2006), Villenas specifically highlighted the raced and gendered experiences of Latina mothers. She focused on the how Latina mothers performed pedagogical moments (Villenas, 2006) in culturally specific ways while at the same time negotiating struggles and oppressions. She found that these experiences were both similar and different to those of Latinas living in traditional gateway states where Latina/o presence is more historically and politically marked. Villenas (2002) found that *educación* in the New Latino Diaspora also disrupted monolithic views on *educación* and child rearing in general. Her work offered an interesting view on the fears and contradictions Latina mothers had and the adjustments they had to make when raising their children where ties to an emerging community were not as strong yet. The inculcation of *educación* as a moral education was underlined by a sense of urgency to instill moral values that the children could abide by while their mothers fulfilled their duties as workers in the factories of Hope City. Villenas and Moreno's (2001) work on Latina mother/daughter relationships in the New Latino Diaspora looked specifically at the education mothers instilled in their daughters. They educated their daughters on being women who are duty bound to certain culturally defined responsibilities such as being *una mujer de hogar* (a woman of the home). However, these mothers also conveyed messages that subverted these same patriarchal systems and taught them through the use of *consejos* to *valerse por si misma,* to be self-reliant and seek more than just a place in the home. North Carolina was at the center of Alma and Blanca's narratives as they each revealed context specific perspectives experiences of space that resulted in a *confianza* or lack-thereof in their communities.

## 4 The Present Study

This project was envisioned as being as an exploration of a mentoring program through the eyes of the Latina mothers of mentees. In my initial review of the data, and subsequent reflection on my interview experience with Alma, I found points of interest that were not fully explored in the first round of interview. From the initial round of interviews, I chose Alma and Blanca to serve as case studies (Patton, 2001). Case studies are useful in that they allow a detailed examination of a particular setting and subject (Bogdan & Biklen, 2003). I conducted a second round of interviews focused on their family relationships, *confianza,* and experiences with the mentoring program. The interviews were semi-structured (Denzin & Lincoln, 1994; Bogdan & Biklen, 2003). I prepared a set of questions to guide the interview, however, I attempted to treat them less like interviews and more like *pláticas*—essentially, relaxed conversations rather than tense interrogations.

### 4.1 Narratives as Method

This study was designed to provide the avenue to document and elucidate these Latina mothers' narratives. By using narratives with a Chicana feminist perspective (Delgado Bernal, 1998; 2001; Elenes, Gonzalez, Delgado Bernal, & Villenas, 2001), I sought to honor the lived experiences of these mothers. Narratives of life experiences are a phenomenon that, if used as a method, can provide critical insight into the complexity of life experiences (Connelly & Clandinin, 1990; Webster & Mertova, 2007). Bell (2002) describes the use of narrative inquiry as

> going beyond the use of narratives as rhetorical structure, that is, simply telling stories, to an analytic examination of the underlying insights and assumptions that the story illustrates. (p. 208)

These narratives can be presented in different ways such as interviews, written narratives, and story telling (Bell, 2002; Xu, Connelly, Fang He, & Philllion, 2007). The interviews presented in this study serve as narratives. I intended for the participants to depict their worlds through their interviews (Webster & Mertova, 2007) and thus construct their own narratives. Webster and Mertova (2007) asserted that narratives do not exist in a vacuum and are shaped by personal experiences as well as community narratives. This aspect of narratives is very important to this work as it seeks to contribute to the literature on Chicana ways of knowing and teaching. Chicana feminist frameworks are informed by community history and knowledge. Just as their pedagogies do not exist in a vacuum, neither do their narratives. Community narratives are also an important part of these Latina mothers' narratives because as part of the New Latino Diaspora, they were creating new communities in spaces that do not have a historical Latina/o presence, thus providing narratives that are unique to new diaspora spaces.

In the researcher/participant relationship, where powers dynamics can favor the researcher, Connelly and Clandinin (1990) assert that in narratives, participants must have a voice in the research relationship and researchers must privilege the participant by centering their narratives because the research power dynamics can silence participants. Historically, Latina/os have been silenced and marginalized in and by academia through uncritical scholarship that fails to acknowledge different raced, gendered, and classed systems of oppression. In doing so, Latina/os are situated as the makers of their own marginalization (Delgado Bernal, 1998; Villenas et al., 2006; Villenas, 2001). Canagarajah (1996) contended that narratives could disrupt the elitist scholarly discourses by offering an opportunity for marginalized groups to participate in knowledge construction. These narratives can be very purposeful in acknowledging and highlighting the local knowledge of the communities and also create knowledge from the grassroots up rather than academia/researcher-imposed theories that go from the top down. Alma and Blanca's narratives can also be used to inform how mentors can address the needs of Latina mentees. I sought to understand each woman's narrative individually before developing "The Pillars of *Confianza*" in which I connect the two narratives. It was important to preserve each woman's point of view and acknowledge the similarities and differences in their interpretations of *confianza*. For example, you will see that in my discussion of *obligación* (under the section titled *Respeto*), Alma and Blanca had two different interpretations of what *obligación* means and its role in *confianza*.

## 4.2 Chicana Feminisms

In their work, Chicana feminist scholars seek to dismantle the historically deficit and peripheral frames that compound the systems of oppression that

Chicanas are subject to (Delgado Bernal, 1998). Chicana feminist theory centers lived experiences and Chicana feminist scholars "theorize ... lived experience as a knowledge base to understand, critique, and challenge system oppression and theorize identity, sexuality, the body, resistance, healing, transformation, and empowerment" (Pérez Huber & Cueva, 2012, p. 395). One way Chicana scholars have done this, is by redefining everyday experiences and culturally specific ways of teaching and knowing as important sources of knowledge and communal knowing (Delgado Bernal, 2001; Villenas, Godinez, Delgado Bernal, & Elenes, 2006). Chicana feminist scholarship has elucidated multiple ways of teaching and knowing amongst Chicanas. They are, to name a few, the concept of *educación, la facultad* (knowing through experience and intuition), *consejos* (narrative advice), *respeto* (respect), and *valerse por si misma* (self reliance) (Villenas et al., 2006; Elenes, Gonzalez, Delgado Bernal, & Villenas, 2001; Valdes, 1996).

Chicana feminist theory is a theory of agency that is woman centered and woman defined. This scholarship frames mothers as central figures to their children's socialization and serve as the conduits through which cultural knowledge is transmitted (Villenas et al., 2006). Taking into account Ream's (2005) assertion that *confianza* is learned through family interactions and coupling this knowledge with Chicana feminist frameworks, this project focuses on how these Latina mothers define and practice *confianza* with their families and communities.

### 4.3    *Cultural Intuition*

It is important for me, as a Chicana researcher employing a Chicana feminist epistemology, to acknowledge the origins of this project. The conceptual idea for this project on *confianza* arose out of the experience of interviewing Alma Martínez, a Mexican immigrant mother, as part of a research team evaluating a mentoring program that Alma's children were a part of. While the content of her interview revealed critical insight into the mentoring program and her experiences with program coordinators and mentors, what struck me most was how we experienced the interviewing process. Here, I give an account of my experiences in the Martínez home and will further explain how I drew the concept of *confianza* out of them.

As one of two native Spanish speakers and the only Chicana member of the evaluation team, one of my most prominent roles was interview the Latina/o parents and their children. By virtue of how potential interviewees were divided amongst the researchers and also by virtue of timing, it was I who ended up recruiting Alma Martínez and her three children for interviews. She

INCULCANDO CONFIANZA                                                      125

gave her permission to interview herself and her children and we arranged for
the interviews to be conducted over a two consecutive day period. Alma, with
her children lined up behind her, greeted me at the door and directed me to
sit in the living room while her children put away their homework. I observed
the family pictures, the eldest daughter's *Quinceañera* portrait and the small
*Virgen de Guadalupe* image above the family laptop—all objects I was familiar
with and accustomed to seeing in my mother's and my grandmothers' homes.
*Platicamos* (we chatted), mostly in Spanish, on the nature of the program evaluation and purpose of the interviews as well as soccer, given that Patrizia, the
youngest, had just arrived from soccer practice. I divulged that while I loved
the sport, I was a very poor player. When I asked who would like to be interviewed first, Alma instructed that I interview her children first and she wanted
to be interviewed last, on the second day. I interviewed Evelyn, the oldest, first
and then Patrizia. It is important to note that both interviews were conducted
in the presence of their mother, who, despite not speaking and understanding
very little English, quietly watched my interactions with her daughters. On the
second night, our greetings were less formal as we were a little more familiar
with each other. Again, *platicamos* a little before I began the interviews. It was
during this *plática,* that we discovered that both of our families were immigrants from the Mexican state of Tamaulipas and I grew up an hour from their
hometown.

> ER: *¿Són de Reynosa? Yo soy de Roma en este lado del río. Mis papás son
> de Cuidad Miguel Alemán. Me encantaba ir a Reynosa.* [You are from
> Reynosa? I am from Roma on this side of the river. My parents are
> from Cuidad Miguel Aleman. I loved going to Reynosa.]
>
> AM: *¿Ahh si? Miguel Alemán no esta tan lejos de Reynosa. Si lo conozco. ¿A
> que te gustaba ir* [*a Reynosa*]*?* [Ahh yes? Miguel Aleman is not far
> from Reynosa. I do know it. Why did you like to go [to Reynosa?]]

We discussed my favorite restaurant in Reynosa and lamented that it in fact
had closed a couple of years back. Before we could continue this conversation,
Evelyn interrupted us to ask me if I thought the actor in the *telenovela* (soap
opera) she was watching was "guapo" (attractive). I responded to her honestly
when I said that I did not and Alma laughed and Evelyn reacted in such a way
that gave me the impression that I might have settled a debate between them.
Still, Evelyn protested that she thought he was "hot."

These interactions, along with the ones from the day before, set the tone
for my interview with Alma. During my interview with Alma, she openly (and

unsolicited) revealed her and her family's undocumented status to me. This was the moment that struck me, as I did not expect her to openly reveal this to a stranger. I am not trying to imply that immigration status is something that one should be ashamed of revealing but in my mind, I had stepped into this home, a complete stranger, representing a research team and my purpose was to interview them about this mentoring program. Alma felt that it was safe to reveal to me this kind of sensitive information. This moment, I believe, was facilitated by the interactions (some of which are described in this section) she had seen me have with her children and herself. I drew on my cultural intuition (Delgado Bernal, 1998) to unpack the meaning of this experience and realized that during this two-day period, we had established a certain level of *confianza.*

To give name to my experiences as a Chicana researcher as well as provide a space for these women to share their narratives, I borrow Delgado Bernal's (1998) work on cultural intuition. Delgado Bernal's (1998) notion of cultural intuition itself draws from Strauss and Corbin's (1990) work on theoretical sensitivity. Theoretical sensitivity refers to researchers being able to use personal experiences as "[an] ability to give meaning to data, [a] capacity to understand, and [a] capability to separate the pertinent from that which isn't" (as quoted in Solórzano & Yosso, 2002, p. 33). Delgado Bernal (1998) extends on theoretical sensitivity by developing the four sources of cultural intuition, which are: Personal experiences, existing literature, professional experience, and analytical research process. Cultural intuition differs from theoretical sensitivity in that Delgado Bernal asserts that personal experiences are shaped by and include collective experiences and community memories and knowledge. Some of the ways community memory and knowledge is passed down include *leyendas, corridos,* storytelling, and behaviors such as *consejos, respeto* and *educación* (Delgado Bernal, 1998). *Educación* is an education on morals, ethics, and values (Valdes, 1996) and Villenas (2001) defined a person with *buena educación* as someone who has proper social skills, is respectful and worthy of respect, and also, someone who has loyalty to their families and communities. My *educación,* largely shaped by my Mexican immigrant mother, along with existing Chicana feminist literature made me sensitive to different and important sources of knowledge. My cultural intuition as a Chicana allowed me to recognize the *confianza* between I, as a researcher, and Alma, as a participant. But "cultural intuition is a complex process that is experiential, intuitive, and dynamic" (Delgado Bernal, 1998, pp. 567–568) and thus, I felt that I could not and should not articulate for these women what *confianza* is and thus, I consciously centered their words and stories in order to unpack the practice.

INCULCANDO CONFIANZA

## 5    Buscando *Confianza*

### 5.1    *Alma*

Alma is an immigrant from the Mexican state of Tamaulipas who came to the Southern U.S. in 2002. Her husband, Roberto Sr., had already been living in the south for a year. His trip to North Carolina was supposed to be temporary, as he had come with the intentions of visiting his brother. However, after being a year away from his family, Roberto Sr. told Alma that North Carolina had more to offer for their children than Reynosa and that instead of him returning to Mexico, she, along with their children—Evelyn (now 17 years old), Roberto Jr. (now 15 years old), and Patrizia (now 11 years old)—should join him in the United States.

> *Allá es mas difícil … no hay beneficios para ayudarnos como aquí. Por eso nos venimos ya que nosotros no pudimos salir adelante por el estudio. [Roberto] pensó mas en [nuestros hijos] para que ellos tuvieran algo mejor que nosotros.*
> [It is more difficult over there … there are not any benefits to help us like there are here. That's why we came, since we could not get ahead with our studies. Roberto thought of our children so they could have something better than us.]

Here, Alma was very clear that the goal of moving the entire family to the United States was to take advantage of the educational opportunities this country could offer to Evelyn, Roberto Jr., and Patrizia.

Alma also revealed that she had a difficult time adjusting to life in the United States. She explained that the linguistic and cultural differences were difficult to navigate and her uneasiness was exasperated by the fact that her oldest daughter, who was seven years old at the time, was also having difficulty with the language at school. Alma had even more difficulty adjusting after her brother in law, the only family member outside her children and husband living in the country and the person most familiar with their new surroundings, decided to move back to Mexico. She said:

> *Nos quedamos solitos. Si estuve muy triste por que yo nunca estuve fuera de Reynosa y del momento que me casé si me separé de mis papás pero vivíamos ahí, cerquita, que cuando nos venimos para acá, si fue muy duro. Hasta lloraba en las noches. Estaba muy triste. Pero me fui adaptando.*
> [We were left alone. I was very sad because I had never been outside of Reynosa and from the moment that I got married, I did separate from my

parents, but we lived right there, so close, that when we came over here, it was very hard. I would even cry at nights. I was so sad. But I started adapting.]

Her adaptation to North Carolina came as a result of establishing some friendships but cites that her biggest motivation for doing so came from seeing that her children were showing signs of being academically successful, especially after the oldest learned more English. *"Empecé a tenerle mas confianza a este lugar"* [I began to trust this place more]. Only through the passage of time and the fact that her Evelyn could help by serving as a translator for her mother, was Alma able to begin to have *confianza* towards her new surroundings. She also saw her sacrifices affirmed by the positive impact the place having on her children.

Communication plays an important role in Alma's relationship with her children. She expressed that her mother had taught her to always be open with her children and talk with them. She conveyed a sense of pride in describing her relationship to all three of her children. Alma, who cleans houses for a living, tried to be home before her youngest, Patrizia, came home from school. If she is not able to make it before then, she described that once she arrives, her children stop whatever it is that they are doing, turn off the television, and sit her in the kitchen to discuss the day. *"Ellos respetan el tiempo que tenemos juntos"* [They respect the time we have together]. Time spent *en convivencia* provided the groundwork necessary to establish the family's systems of support. Jasis and Ordonez-Jasis (2004) described convivencia as "moments of collective creation and solidarity." For this Alma and her family, moments of communal sharing most happened at the kitchen table, through conversations.

> *Mas que nada es para que ellos tengan confianza en mi ... Para mi, mas que todo, es la comunicación. Es por eso que platico mucho con las niñas. Les pregunto que inquietudes tienen, les pregunto de sus amigos, amigas. Al niño igual. Le dije a mi esposo que el se va a encargar de el por que niño pero desgraciadamente, mi esposo, por su trabajo no tiene suficiente para mi niño del modo que también que ya empezó a crecer y también le pregunto que inquietudes tiene y platicamos.*
> [More than anything its so they can have *confianza* in me ... for me, more than anything, it's about communication. That's why I have a lot of conversations with the girls. I ask them about their worries, about their friends. The boy, it's the same. I told my husband that he was going to be in charge of his because he was a boy but unfortunately, my husband, because of his work, he does not have enough time. Now that he is getting older, I also ask him about his worries and we talk.]

INCULCANDO CONFIANZA 129

For Alma, it was important for her children to have *confianza* in her and she laid the groundwork for this by showing interest in their daily lives—by asking. Even with her son, with whom she thought it would be different, she learned that she could have meaningful conversations with him as in the end, it did not matter that he was male and she female because most importantly, they were mother and son.

She also divulged that she had very few friends because

> *hay personas que les gusta estar en el chisme. Yo prefiero retirarme de personas así. Por eso me mantengo mas en mi casa. Por que no me gusta estar escuchando de esta persona o otra. Me gusta estar enfocando en mis hijos, en mi casa.*
>
> [There are people who only like to gossip. I prefer to get away from people like that. That's why I like to keep to my house. Because I do not like hearing about this person or that person. I like to focus on my children, on my home.]

For Alma, gossip was not meaningful communication and she also considered it a poor character trait—one that does not necessarily warrant her *confianza*. Thus, when discussing what *confianza* meant to her, she always referred back to her relationships with her children. For Alma, *confianza* is very much tied to family—it is about familial unity.

When I asked who she had *confianza* towards, outside of her family, and she cited Allison, Evelyn's mentor, as one of the few people she had a lot of *confianza* in. She even described Allison as being part of the family. At the time of the interview, Allison had served as Evelyn's mentor for six years and had solidified her place as a member of the family by becoming Evelyn's *Quinceñera* godmother. Beyond her school-based mentorship, Allison also took on a spiritual guiding role in Evelyn's transition into young womanhood. However, Alma was hesitant to trust Allison at first but both women made an effort to engage and get to know one other in order to establish that *confianza*. According to Alma, Allison showed interest in improving her Spanish in order to better communicate with her, and Allison also accepted invitations to spend time with the family as a whole (making *tamales,* attending birthday parties, and Christmas celebrations) rather than limiting her interactions to only Evelyn.

In summary, for Alma, establishing and maintaining *confianza* was of utmost importance for the relationship between herself and her children. She noted that *confianza* "*es para que uno se sienta seguro de esa persona ... mas que nada, la seguridad. Le tiene que dar confianza por conociéndola, tratándola*" [it's so one can feel secure ... more than anything, its security. You give *confianza* by knowing a person, interacting with a person]. In Alma's case, *confianza* was constantly being (re)affirmed by partaking in moments of solidarity and communication and she did express security in knowing that her children not only respected their time together but also respected their mother even when they were not in her presence. These forms of respect and solidarity were also echoed in her relationship with Evelyn's mentor, Allison.

## 5.2    *Blanca*

Blanca, an immigrant from Colombia, came to North Carolina via New York City 16 years prior to her participation in this study. Blanca and her husband, Alberto—an immigrant from Guanajuato, Mexico—have three children, Lucía (17 years old), Eduardo (11 years old) and Gabriela (5 years old). Blanca and Alberto chose to move to North Carolina because, at the time, Alberto's sister also lived there. However, once Blanca's sister in law moved away, like Alma, Blanca did not have any other family living in the area. Blanca described feeling culture shocked when they first moved to North Carolina because while they had been used to a bigger number of Latina/os living in New York City, they now found themselves in an area where there were not only few Latina/os at the time, but the town was also relatively new to Latina/o migration. She remembered feeling stressed because of the language differences but her anxieties were soon soothed their new small town. "*Después nos gustó mucho porque aquí, la ayuda que dan para los hijos, el ambiente para la familia, no es comparable a lo de Nueva York. Entonces fue lo que mas nos gusto*" [Afterwards, we liked it a lot because here, the help that is given for the children, the environment for the family, you can't compare it to New York. That is what we liked the most]. In fact, both Blanca and Alma cited how *calmado* this small town was for raising children. At the same time, however, Blanca did not feel as welcomed to the space and expressed that she had been living in North Carolina long enough to sense a shift in sentiment towards Latina/os.

> *Cuando nosotros llegamos primero aquí, no quiero decir que la gente es mas grosera ahora pero años atrás era súper amable, súper cordial. Yo me acuerdo que me decían hola y hasta me volteaba para ver a quien le hablaban pero me daba cuenta que era a mi ... Pero a cambiando un poquito. No se que paso, pero si a cambiando. Hay gente que es mas racista ... pienso que es por que hay mas Latinos.*
> [When we first got here, I don't want to say that people are more rude today but years ago they were super amiable, super cordial. I remember that people used to say hi and I would even turn around to see who they

were talking about but I realized they were talking to me ... But it has changed a little. I do not know why but it has changed. There are more racist people ... I think it's because there are more Latinos.]

The realization that with greater numbers comes more awareness of and resistance to Latina/os was of particular importance to Blanca because she too, then, became aware of racism. She told a story of an experience with a racist gas station attendant who, upon listening to them speak Spanish, told Blanca and her co-workers that they should not speak Spanish because they were living in America. While her co-workers were visibly distraught and cried in the vehicle, Blanca told them that they should ignore that gas attendant and should continue to speak however they want, wherever they want. Blanca's refusal to be shamed at that moment highlights why it's so important for her children to maintain the Spanish language. Her oldest daughter, in her first years of adolescence, began to refuse to speak Spanish and denounced it as an ugly language. Blanca blamed other children in the schools for putting those ideas in Lucía's head. But Blanca was pro-active in her desire for her children to continue speaking Spanish. In her efforts to ensure that Gabriela, her youngest child, would not suffer from the same internalized oppressions and possibly limit her exposure to negative language ideologies that privilege the English language, Blanca placed her in a Spanish language daycare and had plans to transfer her to a dual language school once she entered the first grade. She also revealed that speaking English and watching English language television was prohibited in her home, and that the family language was and would always be Spanish.

For Blanca, the most important reason for why her children needed maintain the Spanish language was so they could communicate meaningfully with each other. When asked what was important to her and her relationship with Lucía, Alberto, and Gabriela was communication.

> *Para nosotros es muy importante el hablar. Hablar, hablar, y hablar. Para aconsejarlos. Para enseñarles a ser amable, que no hagan* bully. *Para aconsejarlos que estudien mucho para que no tengan que trabajar duro como nosotros. Yo limpio casas y mi esposo el* manager *de mantenimiento de unos apartamentos. Ese trabajo es bien pesado.*
> [For us, it's really important to talk. Talk, talk, and talk. So we can give them advice. So we can teach them to be amiable, that they should no bully. So we can advise them to study a lot so they do not have to work hard like we do. I clean houses and my husband is an apartment maintenance manager. This kind of work is really heavy.]

Blanca, who did not speak English, sarcastically said "*desafortunadamente para ellos tienen papas hispanos y nosotros hablamos el español*" [Unfortunately for them, they have Hispanic parents and we speak Spanish]. Also, it was important for Blanca to use her and her husband's stories of struggle and *sacrificio* (sacrifice) as the foundation for the *educación* of their children. This was done through the use of *consejos*—narrative advice—as well as taking Lucía, who, at the time, thinking about colleges, to clean houses with her to that her daughter actually experience what her mother would talk to her about. To Blanca, this kind of communication was one of the most important to have.

In describing what *confianza* meant to her, Blanca found it easier to derive meaning through telling me the story of how one can lose *confianza*.

> *Lucía tuvo una etapa súper difícil. Era muy rebelde. Mi esposo y yo tuvimos muchos problemas. Ella me atacaba mas a mi. Entonces yo me aleje de ella. Ella me decía 'es que tu no me quieres, nunca me dices' ... le dije que 'es que yo ya no te tengo confianza por que me has atacado tanto ... esa confianza te la tienes que volver a ganar por que yo estoy desilusionada en ti.' Entonces, ya habla mas conmigo. Se a ganado mi confianza.*
> [Lucia went through a stage that was very difficult. She was very rebellious. My husband and I had a lot of problems. She would attack me more. So then, I distanced myself from her. She would tell me 'you don't love me, you never tell me you do' ... I told her 'it's that I no longer have *confianza* in you because you have attacked me so much ... you have to earn my *confianza* again because I am disillusioned in you.' Now she talks to me more. She has earned my *confianza*.]

Blanca's description is interesting because whereas Alma talked about what she had to do for her children to have *confianza* in her, Blanca described it as what her daughter had to do to earn her mother's *confianza* and emphasized what one has to do to prove themselves worthy of *confianza*. This was not limited to her children, however. She described Marisa, her best friend and someone whom she has complete *confianza* towards, as someone who, through actions, has proven herself not only worthy of friendship but of *confianza*. Blanca divulged that she has learned to be very selective with her friendships because she had experienced various forms of betrayal at the hands of people she thought were her friends. However, Marisa, whom she has been friends with for seven years, is someone who Blanca can feel she can "*desahogarse*," someone she can vent to and talk about issues, particularly those involving her side of the family, that she does not feel comfortable sharing with her husband. "Ella *a estado ahí en las buenas y en las malas.*"[*She* has been there in

INCULCANDO CONFIANZA

the good, and in the bad.] She gave the example of when she had surgery the year before, Marisa not only visited her in the hospital, but helped care for her during recovery. No other friend, she said, was willing to do that for her.

She also spoke very highly of her Lucía's mentor, Iris.

> *Iris sabe todo de la vida de mi hija. Iris me ha visto llorar. A sido mi paño de lagrimas. A respecto a de mi hija, si se la quiere llevar, se la puede llevar. Le tengo toda la confianza. Se que es responsable.*
> [Iris knows everything about my daughter's life. Iris has seen me cry. She has been the cloth to my tears. In terms of my daughter, if she wants to take her somewhere, she can take her. I have all the *confianza* in her. I know she is responsible.]

For Blanca, however, her *confianza* in Iris was (re)affirmed by Iris's respect of Blanca's rules and expectations. The mentor and the parent must not only be aligned with one another but the mentor must cede to the parent's expectations. Blanca also came to view Iris as an aunt for Lucía, a particularly important role as Iris did not have adult female relatives living in town. In her interview, Blanca showed how and why *confianza* was lost and to a certain extent what one has to do (re)gain *confianza*. For her, *confianza* was about showing love through respect.

> *Yo siempre he dicho que los hijos, el matrimonio, y las amistades son como una planta. Si la cuidas, la alimentas, le das cariño, ¿qué te va a dar? Mucho fruto, hojas brillantes. Si no la cuidas, esa planta se marchita y se va a morir. Eso es lo que pasa con uno. Uno se va marchitando ... tienes que querer tener esa confianza. Que trabajar por ella.*
> [I have always said that our children, marriage, and friendships are like a plant. If you take care of it, you feeds it, you care for it, what is it going to give you? A lot of fruit, brilliant leaves. If you do not take care of it, that plan will wither and die. That is what can happen to a person. A person will begin to wither ... you have to want to have that *confianza*. You have to work for it.]

## 6      The Pillars of Confianza

Alma and Blanca differed, at some points, in how they interpreted and operationalized *confianza*. However, they did point to some common themes themes in their practice and teaching of *confianza*. In my analysis of Alma and Blanca's

134                                                                    RODRIGUEZ

narratives, I identified three pillars that are key to establishing and sustaining *confianza: convivencia* (communal coexistence), *respeto* (respect) and *cariño* (affection). Below, I describe and, define each pillar and discuss how it related to *confianza*.

### 6.1    *Convivencia*

For both Alma and Blanca, time spent together as a family was of utmost importance. Most of the (re)affirmations of support and *confianza* for one another happened sitting around the kitchen table talking. According to their narratives, for these mothers, conversations about friends, school, insecurities, and even chores also served as moments of teaching and learning—mainly through the use of *consejos,* which Delgado-Gaitan (1994) defined as cultural narratives of advice. For Blanca, *convivencia* provided stability for her family, stability necessary for her there to be *confianza* amongst each other. "*Necesitamos estas unidos. Si los padres están acá arriba, los hijos también tienen que estar arriba ... hay que tener una firmesa en el matrimonio, en familia, para que los hijos te tengan confianza*" [We need to be united. If the parents are on top, the children also need to be on top ... there had to be a firmness in the marriage, in the family, so that the children can have *confianza* in you].She described using games to inspire family unity and to bridge the top-down gap that can exist between parents and their children.

Both women expressed that in order to have *confianza* towards someone, they had to know the person very well—to know their character. One of the reason's Alma had such few friendships and could not necessarily name many people she could trust was because through time spent with some of these women, she got to know their behaviors and their beliefs. As aforementioned, for Alma, gossiping was a poor character trait and she lost respect for women who constantly engaged in it. Blanca had a similar experience when spending time with friends she does not necessary have *confianza* in. The most important point of this, is that these women were also able to determine who was and was not worth of having their *confianza* by spending time with them. The only way to truly get to know someone is to *convivir* with them. Alma stated:

> *Necesita uno conocer [a la persona] ver si le tiene confianza o no ... pero es muy difícil que yo le tenga confianza a alguien. Pasaría mucho tiempo para que yo tenga confianza ... necesitaría ver como es esa persona. Si es reservada como yo. No le gusta a andar para allá y para acá.*
> [You need to know the person to see if you can have *confianza* or not ... but it's difficult for me to have confianza in someone. A lot of time would

INCULCANDO CONFIANZA 135

need to pass so I can have *confianza* … I would need to see how that person is. If they are reserved like me. That they do not like to be going here and there.]

In this excerpt, Alma also made an interesting point about compatibility and being able to recognize herself, her morals, and values in others. In her interview on mentoring, Alma revealed that she did not trust Allison at first. She was hesitant to let her then 11 year old daughter go anywhere with Allison. But in time, the women got to know each other and Alma cited that they both hold similar values—especially when it came to their goals for Evelyn. Allison supported Alma by expecting and helping Evelyn to achieve high academic success. *Convivencia* is not just about being in the same space but it is also about communal sharing of thoughts, ideas, and time. Time spent in *convivencia* between Alma and Allison played an important role in establishing and maintaining *confianza* between both of these women—especially for Alma who is hesitant to *confiar* in anyone outside of her family. Allison also furthered her studies in Spanish in order to have better communication with Alma as well as visited with the entire family in addition to assembling *tamales* at the kitchen table.

## 6.2 *Respeto*

*La diferencia cuando una persona tiene esa confianza en ti, te respeta, te admira,. Todo esta unido. Si tu respetas, las persona te va tener la confianza total.*
[The difference is that when has that *confianza* in you, they will respect you, they will admire you. Everything is united. If you respect, that person will have total *confianza* in you.] (Alma)

Like *convivencia,* Valdes (1996), argues that the notion of *respeto* is a concept that is not fully encompassed by its English translation (respect). She argued that

*respeto* in its broadest sense is a set of attitudes toward individuals and/ or the roles that they occupy. It is believed that certain roles demand or require particular types of behavior … it is especially significant among members of the family. Having *respeto* for one's family involves functioning according to specific views about the nature of the roles filled by various members of the family …. It involved demonstrating personal regard for the individual. (Valdes, 1996, p. 130)

Both Alma and Blanca, cited *respeto* as being one of the most important lessons they taught (and were still teaching) their children. One aspect of *respeto* in terms of *confianza* is how Alma described her and her son's manners. She taught her children *respeto* mainly through example— by honoring her responsibilities and treating others cordially. She expressed that, in particular, she was very *orgullosa* (proud) of Roberto Jr. because his friends' parents often commented to her about how he was always very respectful and cordial. "Me *siento admirada mucho de eso porque así saben que le pueden tener confianza a mi hijo*" [I feel admired because of that because now they know that they can trust him]. She felt Roberto Jr.'s manners and how he presented himself to his friends' parents led them to trust him. This could be because she felt his *respeto* towards adults is an indicator of good character. Blanca expressed a similar sentiment when she described how she required her children to address adults as *señor* or *señora*. Formality was also another sign of a *buena educación* (a good moral education).

Another incarnation of *respeto* within the concept of *confianza* is the idea of *obligaciónes* (obligations) and reciprocity. Alma and Blanca both differed on the role *obligación* had in their definitions of *confianza*. In describing her *obligaciones* to her family, Blanca expressed that she had to fulfill her duties as a wife and mother everyday. Among the most important of her duties, was showing her family that she respected them. For example, both Blanca and her husband gave Lucía their permission for her to have a boyfriend. Her husband, however, showed a great dislike for the young man and constantly made remarks to Lucía. Blanca took it upon herself to instruct her husband to respect the fact that he had given his permission for Lucía to date this particular boy and to also respect her choice of boyfriend. "*No lo tiene que querer, pero si tiene que respetar como padre*" [He does not have to love him, but he does have to respect as a father]. Here she designated that their roles as parents, their obligations as parents, were to support and respect their daughter and give her space to make her own decisions. This is an example of Blanca showing that she both had *confianza* that her daughter would make the right decision, as well as reaffirmed to Lucía that her mother was also someone worth exhibiting *confianza* towards. Also, for Blanca, there were clear behaviors her children had to exhibit in order to warrant giving her *confianza* to them. For example, the story about her issues with Lucía showed that in Blanca's eyes Lucía was not treated her with the level of *respeto* a child was supposed to afford to her mother. Lucía would raise her voice, insult Blanca, and made accusations towards her. This behavior pushed Blanca away and resulted in her losing a great amount of *confianza* towards her daughter. Alma, on the other hand, rejected the idea of *obligaciones* as she wanted her children to do the right

INCULCANDO CONFIANZA 137

thing because they wanted to—for them to have an inner desire to fulfill their responsibilities. While for Alma *obligación* had the connotation that her children were being forced to act in certain ways, the inner desire she described was in line with the idea that her children knew what was expected of them and because of their *educación* and *respeto* towards their parents, wanted to fulfill those duties. It was her *educación* and pedagogies in actions.

In respect to mentorship, both women noted that mentors had an *obligación* to be with and guide their daughters. This *obligación* was solidfied by establishing familial bonds with the mentors. Blanca viewed Iris as another aunt for Lucía, while Allison actually became part of the family unit as Evelyn's godmother. By establishing these familial bonds, the women not only gave the mentors a place in their home, but also extended some of the expectations that come with a strong emphasis on familism like respect and honoring one's role and duty to the family not just the mentee.

Responsibleness is another way of identifying whether or not to have *confianza* in someone. Blanca's discussion of responsibility differs from her discussion of *obligación* in that she spoke specifically about Iris's responsibility as a mentor to Lucía. But it was not necessarily responsibility in completely certain tasks but in Iris's regard towards Alma and her husband as Lucía's parents.

> *Una persona responsable, siempre he dicho, tiene que ser una persona honesta. Por que el que no es responsable, no le va a importar nada. La persona que es responsable se va a preocupar por que va a decir 'o que dirán los papás si yo no llego a tiempo.' Esa persona va a cuidar lo que uno piensa de ellos.*
> [A responsible person, I have always said, has to be an honest person. Because those are not responsible are not going to care about anything. The person that is responsible is going to worry because they will say 'oh what would the parents think if I do not get back on time.' That person is going care about what we think about them.]

For the mentor relationship to be right and effective for the children, the mentor's relations must be right with the parents' as well. Iris's apparent *respeto* and regard for Blanca is one of the reasons why Blanca feels it's okay to exhibit *confianza* towards her. She trusts Iris will take care of her daughter, respect her rules, and most importantly, she trusts Iris will provide Blanca the help she is meant to give.

## 6.3    *Cariño*

The third pillar of *confianza* is *cariño*. *Cariño* refers to the love and affection that characterize a relationship with *confianza*. Alma and Blanca were both very forthcoming with the fact that they did not have *confianza* in many people outside of their family. In fact, they were cautious in investing in people whom they did not trust. This led me to conclude that those relationships that do have *confianza,* are prioritized over others. Therefore, these relationships and the *confianza* that characterizes them must be nurtured by showing *cariño*.

In these mother-child relationships, *cariño* was by being honest and open with their children. When Lucía began dating her boyfriend, Blanca had a conversation with Lucía about the possibility of her becoming sexually active. Blanca told me that her goals in having this conversation with her daughter were to show her daughter that she does not judge her so that when the time comes, Lucía can trust her mother enough to be open her. "Quería *que supiera que yo estoy aquí para darle apoyo. Yo la llevo al doctor para tomar todas las precauciones"* [I wanted her to know that I am here to support her. I will take her to the doctor so she can take all the precautions]. In this case, Blanca approached the situation calmly and from a genuine place of love.

*Cariño* is also about solidarity. As mentioned in her narrative, Iris showed *cariño* when she comforted Blanca through some of the most contentious and painful moments in the relationship with her daughter. Even though Iris was technically not there to provide this emotional support for her mentee's mother, she still fulfilled that role because they had established a connection beyond mentoring and the mentoring program. For both women, it was important to establish a familial bond with the mentors. This familial bond meant showing and knowing that both parties are invested in growing, protecting, and re-affirming their commitments to the mentoring/family relationships. *Cariño* is also about honoring, accepting, and loving people for who they are.

## 7 Possibilities for the Mentorship of Latina Youth

How can these mothers' pedagogies about *confianza* inform mentoring practices and blur the boundaries delineated by the mentoring program? Both Alma and Blanca situated the mentors as family members. Familism is an important and valuable cultural capital for Latina/o families (Valdes, 1996). This signaled that the mothers came to understand mentoring and its possibilities beyond just the social mobility of their children. By becoming family, the mentor took on an *obligación* to the mentee *and* the family. However, these characterizations often conflicted with how the mentors saw themselves. While these mothers saw the mentors as an extension of the family unit, and mentors understood their responsibilities of the mentee and their families, they saw themselves just as mentors. For example, Iris characterized her interactions with 17-year-old

INCULCANDO CONFIANZA

Lucía as an "adult-child" relationship with clear boundaries. She described Lucía as acting "too comfortable" by asking things should shouldn't. (Iris never clarified what subjects were "too much"). While this made Iris uncomfortable, she was still negotiating this discomfort. "It made me uncomfortable ... but again, that's all me and me having to get adjusted." Iris understood, to a certain extent, that despite her feelings on these situations, she had an *obligación* to adjust to her mentee's needs. Interestingly, though, Iris did feel a need to change certain aspects of Lucía like her propensity to ask for advice. "She is always seeking advice so I think I got to try to get her to think more on her own." This is in line with the liberal value of individualism. As noted earlier, Latina female knowledge is co-constructed and passed down through *consejos* (advice). While it might be problematic for Iris that her mentee seeks her guidance *too much,* this not only speaks to the value placed on the knowledge she has to offer, but her mentee is also attempting to operationalize the pedagogies she has learned from her mother. Perhaps unwittingly, Lucía and Iris had established a relationship that empowered the mentee to ask questions she was "not supposed to." Even though this made the mentor uncomfortable, it echoes Brown's (2006) arguments that mentoring should serve to create empowering connections and challenge traditional power relations. When asked what she had learned from her mentee, the first response that Allison offered was that Evelyn had taught her to follow through in her responsibilities as a mentor. " She taught me to follow through. To do what I say and be who I say I am ... Because I wasn't going anywhere. You know, I was committed to being her mentor ... it was all me." This lesson echoes the lessons delineated what constitutes *confianza*. Accountability, respect, and to an extent, *cariño*, were driving Allison's commitment to the mentoring relationship.

In order to tap into the transformative potential of mentoring relationships, mentors must act as partners with their mentees. In her work on mentoring urban girls, Sullivan (1996) argues that healthy mentoring relationships with urban girls are "overwhelmingly characterized by women's ability to listen, understand, and validate knowledge, experiences, and feelings of the adolescent" (p. 226). An adolescent girl's freedom to speak should be accompanied by a mentor's freedom "to listen without need to change them" (p. 24). Brown (2006) contends that in order to create empowering connections between girls and the women who mentor them, mentors must actively work to redefine power relations.

Thus, mentorships that seed power for young Latinas and their families should seek to break down dichotomies or, at the very least, complicate them. It is because of these fluid, relational roles that the boundaries in the relationships described in this piece (between mentee/mentor/mother) are more complex than the mentoring relationship the program sought to delineate. In fact, the idea of drawing boundaries was an important component of new mentor training. Mentoring training sessions stressed the importance of maintaining distance between the mentor, mentee, and the family. While one message spoke to the dangers of overstepping one's role by making assumptions of what the child does and does not need—which falls under the respect one has for the child's culture and parent expectations—demonstrations like a "Rope Exercise" warned of the dangers that come with the mentor sharing too much of themselves. In this demonstration, trainers used a short rope to illustrate what would happen to the relationship if the mentor allowed the mentee (or the family) to *take* too much from or take advantage of the mentor. If this should happen, the rope would become tight and strained to the point of breaking. While I am not arguing that mentoring relationships should not have boundaries, I do note that some of the boundaries delineated by the program are incongruent to how these positive relationships flourished.

Valenzuela (1999) argued that immigrant and U.S. born Mexican youth "are committed to an *authentic* form of caring that emphasizes relations of reciprocity ..." (p. 61). While, in this case Valenzuela was talking about student/teacher relationships, the notion of authentic caring and the emphasis on reciprocity can be applied to my discussion of *confianza*. As these mothers have demonstrated, you cannot trust someone who does not care for you or your wellbeing. You cannot trust someone who does not respect you. You cannot trust someone who you do not know. Blanca poignantly stated: "donde *hay confianza, hay todo*" [Where there is *confianza,* there is everything]. The possibilities of establishing, nurturing, and sustaining relationships based on confianza are endless; on the other side, however, as some of the narratives have revealed, the loss of *confianza* can very detrimental to effectiveness of a relationship.

### 7.1 Towards a Sacred Space of Mentoring

I push that we employ a new framework for the mentorship of young Latinas. I argue that mentoring relationships between mentors, Latinas, and—by extension—their families not only be dialogic in nature but also, actively center Latina women's ways of knowing. In centering Latina epistemologies, the mentoring relationship enters a decolonizing process that demands that issues of power, race, racism, gender, and class not only be acknowledged but also resisted. I wish to borrow from Diaz Soto, Cervantes-Soon, Villareal, and Campos's (2009) model for Xicana Sacred Spaced (XSS) to inform the framework I am beginning to imagine for the mentoring of Latina youth.

Inherently, the mentor/mentee titles denote a top-down approach of knowledge exchange—mainly that the ment*or* gives while the ment*ee* receives. XSS,

INCULCANDO CONFIANZA

on the other hand, places an emphasis on a "circular rather than linear process of knowledge ... [and functions] as an ongoing circle of knowledge sharing" (p. 764). A sacred space of mentoring should be dialogic and reflexive. However, beyond engaging in politics of niceness and safety, like xss, a sacred space of mentoring should not simply be a " 'friendly' space but a space for rigorous exchange of ideas, one impacted by the different subjectivities, standpoints, and histories" (Calderón, Delgado Bernal, Pérez Huber, Malagón, & Velez, 2012, p. 519) of the mentee *and* mentor. That exchange would naturally include the mentee's familial knowledge. Just as the authors described their classroom experience and emergence of xss, tensions and contradictions are inherently part of the mentorship of young women of color. Thus, the purpose of this paper goes beyond rethinking who can inform mentoring practices. It also serves to push towards re-imagining mentoring as a practice. There should be an exchange of knowledge, *respeto, cariño*, and a striving to be in *convicencia,* however, these actions need to have a purpose beyond neo-liberal conceptions of success. It should be an emancipatory and decolonial process for those involved in the mentoring *exchange*. It should push to break down mentor/ mentee binaries and instead put these women in dialogue with each other and in dialogue with the world and the systems that govern it.

The mentoring relationships in this text are complex and transgress the perceived ideas of what makes an effective mentoring exchange. We have seen instances where the mentor/mentee relationship acted beyond the mentor/ mentee parameters. We saw women become friends, aunts, godmothers, teachers and partners in the establishment and sustainment of meaningful relationships. Engaging the pedagogies of the home (Delgado Bernal, 2001) and deliberating creating emancipatory goals can lay the groundwork for the emergence of the sacred space of mentoring. Sharing this space in *confianza* has the possibility to transform mentoring from a practice to a transformative and emancipatory exchange.

### References

Bell, J. S. (2002). Narrative inquiry: More than just telling stories. *TESOL Quarterly, 36*(2), 207–213.

Bernal, D. D. (2002). Critical race theory, Latino critical theory, and critical raced-gendered epistemologies: Recognizing students of color as holders and creators of knowledge. *Qualitative Inquiry, 8*(1), 105–126.

Bogdan, R. C., & Biklen, S. K. (2003). *Qualitative research for education: An introduction to theories and methods.* London: Pearson Education Group, Inc.

Brown, R. N. (2006). Mentoring on the borderlands: Creating empowering connections between adolescent girls and young women volunteers. *Journal of the Sociology of Self-Knowledge, 4*(3), 105–121.

Calderón, D., Bernal, D. D., Huber, L. P., Malagón, M. C., & Vélez, V. N. (2012). A Chicana feminist epistemology revisited: Cultivating ideas a generation later. *Harvard Educational Review, 82*(4), 513–539.

Canagarajah, A. S. (1996). From critical research practice to critical research reporting. *TESOL Quarterly, 30*(2), 321–331.

Carrillo, J. F., & Rodríguez, E. (2016). She doesn't even act Mexican: Smartness Trespassing in the New South. *Race, Ethnicity, and Education, 19*(6), 1236–1246.

Connelly, F. M., & Clandinin, D. J. (1990). Stories of experience and narrative inquiry. *Educational Reviewer, 19*(5), 555–582.

De Leon, B. (1996). Career development of Hispanic adolescent girls. In B. J. Ross Leadbeater & N. Way (Eds.), *Urban girls: Resisting stereotypes, creating identities* (pp. 380–397). New York, NY: New York University.

Delgado Bernal, D. (1998). Using a Chicana feminist epistemology in educational research. *Harvard Educational Review, 68*(4), 555–582.

Delgado Bernal, D. (2001). Learning and living pedagogies of the home: The Mestiza consciousness of Chicana students. *International Journal of Qualitative Studies in Education, 14*(5), 623–639.

Delgado Bernal, D. (2002). Critical race theory, Latino critical theory, and critical raced-gendered epistemologies: Recognizing students of color as holders and creators of knowledge. *Qualitative Inquiry, 8*(1), 105–126.

Delgado-Gaitan, C. (1994). Consejos: The power of cultural narratives. *Anthropology & Education Quarterly, 25*(3), 298–316.

Denner, J., & Guzman, B. L. (2006). Introduction: Latina girls transforming cultures, contexts, and selves. In J. Denner & B. L. Guzman (Eds.), *Latina girls: Voices of adolescent strength in the United States* (pp. 1–16). New York, NY: New York University Press.

Denzin, N. K., & Lincoln, Y. S. (1994). Introduction: Entering the field of qualitative research. In N. K. Denzin & Y. S. Lincoln (Eds.), *Handbook of qualitative research* (pp. 1–17). Thousand Oaks, CA: Sage Publications.

Diaz Soto, L., Cervantes-Soon, C. G., Villarreal, E., & Campos, E. E. (2009). The Xicana sacred space: A communal circle of compromiso for educational researchers. *Harvard Educational Review, 79*(4), 755–776.

Elenes, C. A., Gonzalez, F. E., Delgado Bernal, D., & Villenas, S. (2001). Introduction: Chicana/Mexicana feminist pedagogies: Consejos, respeto, y educación in everyday life. *International Journal of Qualitative Studies in Education, 14*(5), 595–602.

Furuseth, O. J., & Smith, H. A. (2006). From Winn-Dixie to tiendas: The remaking of the new South. In H. A. Smith & O. J. Furuseth (Eds.), *Latinos in the New South transformations of place* (pp. 1–17). Burlington, VT: Ashgate Publishing.

INCULCANDO CONFIANZA 143

Gonzalez, N., Moll, L. C., Tenery, M. F., Rivera, A., Rendon, P., Gonzales, R., & Amanti, C. (1995). Funds of knowledge for teaching in Latino households. *Urban Education, 29*(4), 443–470.

Hamann, E. T., & Harklau, L. (2010) Education in the new Latino diaspora. In E. G. Murillo Jr., S. A. Villenas, R. Trinidad Galvan, J. Sanchez Munoz, C. Martinez, M. Machado-Casas (Eds.), *Handbook of Latinos and education: Research, theory, and practice* (pp. 157–169). New York, NY: Lawrence Erlbaum Routledge.

Hamann, E. T., Wortham, S., & Murillo Jr., E. G. (2002). Education and policy in the new Latino diaspora. In S. Wortham, E. G. Murillo, Jr., & E. T. Hamann (Eds.), *Education in the new Latino diaspora: Policy and politics of identity* (pp. 1–16). Westport, CT: Praeger.

Jasis, P., & Ordonez-Jasis, R. (2004). Convivencia to empowerment: Latino parent organizing at la familia. *The High School Journal, 88*(2), 32–42.

Liang, B., & Grossman, J. M. (2010). Diversity and youth mentoring relationships. In T. D. Allen & L. T. Eby (Eds.), *The blackwell handbook of mentoring: A multiple perspectives approach* (pp. 239–258). Malden, MA: Blackwell Publishing Ltd.

Lopez, N., & Lechuga, C. E. (2007). "They are like a friend": Othermothers creating empowering school based community living rooms in Latina and Latino middle schools. In B. J. Ross Leadbeater & N. Way (Eds.), *Urban girls revisited: Building strengths*. New York, NY: New York University Press.

McLean Taylor, J, Veloria, C. N., & Verba, M. C. (2007). "We are like sisters—most times!" In B. J. Ross Leadbeater & N. Way (Eds.), *Urban girls revisited: Building strengths*. New York, NY: New York University Press.

Moll, L. C., Amanti, C., Neff, D., & Gonzalez, N. (1992). Funds of knowledge for teaching: Using a qualitative approach to connect homes and classrooms. *Theory into Practice, 31*(2), 132–141.

Murillo Jr., E. G. (2002). How does it feel to be a problem?: "Disciplining" the transnational subject in the American south. In S. Wortham, E. G. Murillo Jr., & E. T. Hamann (Eds.), *Education in the new Latino diaspora: Policy and politics of identity* (pp. 215–224). Wesport, CT: Praeger.

Patton, M. Q. (2001). *Qualitative research and evaluation methods*. Thousand Oaks, CA: Sage Publications.

Perez Huber, L., & Cueva, B. M. (2012). Chicana/Latina testimonios on effects and responses to microaggressions. *Equity & Excellence in Education, 45*(3), 392–410.

Quarles, A., Maldonado, N., & Lacey, C. H. (2005, April 1). *Mentoring and at-risk adolescent girls: A phenomenological investigation* (pp. 1–15). Montreal, CA: American Educational Research Association.

Ream, R. K. (2005). Toward understanding how social capital mediates the impact of mobility on Mexican American achievement. *Social Forces, 84*(1), 201–224.

Salguero, C., & McCusker, W. R. (1996). Sympton expression in inner city-Latinas: Psychopathy or help seeking? In B. J. Ross Leadbeater & N. Way (Eds.), *Urban girls: Resisting stereotypes, creating identities* (pp. 328–335). New York, NY: New York University Press.

Solórzano, D. G., & Yosso, T. J. (2002). Critical race methodology: Counter-storytelling as an analytical framework for education research. *Qualitative Inquiry, 8*(23), 23–44.

Stanton-Salazar, R. D. (2001). *Manufacturing hope and despair: The school and kin support networks of US-Mexican youth.* New York, NY: Teachers College Press.

Stanton-Salazar, R. D., & Urso-Spina, S. (2003). Informal mentors and role models in the lives of urban Mexican origin adolescents. *Anthropology & Education Quarterly, 34*(3), 231–254.

Strauss, A., & Corbin, J. (1990). *Basics of qualitative research: Grounded theory procedures and techniques.* Newbury Park, CA: Sage Publications.

Sullivan, A. M. (1996). From mentor to muse: Recasting the role of women in relationship with urban adolescent girls. In B. J. Ross Leadbeater & N. Way (Eds.), *Urban girls: Resisting stereotypes, creating identities* (pp. 226–254). New York, NY: New York University Press.

Valdes, G. (1996). *Con respeto: Bridging the distances between culturally diverse families and schools.* New York, NY: Teachers College Press.

Valenzuela, A. (1999). *U.S.-Mexican youth and the politics of caring.* Albany, NY: State University of New York Press.

Villenas, S. (2001). Latina mothers and small town racisms: Creating narratives of dignity and moral education in North Carolina. *Anthropology & Education Quarterly, 32*(1), 3–28.

Villenas, S. (2002). Reinventing educación in new Latino communities: Pedagogies of change and continuity in North Carolina. In S. Wortham, E. G. Murillo Jr., & E. T. Hamann (Eds.), *Education in the new Latino diaspora: Policy and politics of identity* (pp. 17–36). Wesport, CT: Praeger.

Villenas, S. (2006). Pedagogical moments in the borderlands: Latina mothers teaching and learning. In D. Delgado Bernal, C. A. Elenes, F. E. Godinez, & S. Villenas (Eds.), *Chicana/Latina education in everyday life. Feminista perspectives on pedagogy and epistemology* (pp. 147–160). Albany: State University of New York Press.

Villenas, S., Godinez, F., Bernal, D. D., & Elenes, C. A. (2006). Chicanas/Latinas building bridges: Introduction. In D. Delgado Bernal, C. A. Elenes, F. E. Godinez, & S. Villenas (Eds.), *Chicana/Latina education in everyday life. Feminista perspectives on pedagogy and epistemology* (pp. 1–9). Albany, NY: State University of New York Press.

Villenas, S., & Moreno, M. (2001). To valerse por si misma between race, capitalism, and patriarchy: Latina mother-daughter pedagogies in North Carolina. *International Journal of Qualitative Studies in Education, 14*(5), 671–687.

Webster, L., & Mertova, P. (2007). *Using narrative inquiry as a research method: An introduction to using critical event narrative analysis in research on learning and teaching.* New York, NY: Routledge.

Xu, S., Connelly, F. M., Fang He, M., & Phillion, J. (2007). Immigrant students' experience of schooling: A narrative inquiry theoretical framework. *Journal of Curriculum Studies, 39*(4), 399–422.

CHAPTER 6

# Examining the Mentoring Discourse Regarding the Parenting Practices of Black, Female-Led Families

*Dana Griffin*

## 1 Introduction

The benefits of youth mentoring have been well documented in the literature. For example, youth mentoring has been demonstrated to be an effective strategy in increasing youth competencies and reducing problem behaviors (DuBois, Holloway, Valentine, & Cooper, 2002; LoSciuto, Rajala, Townsend, & Taylor, 1996; Tierney, Grossman, & Resch, 1995). DuBois and Silverthorn (2005) found that adolescents who were part of mentoring relationships had better education and work outcomes. However, more research is needed on the exploration of the impact of youth mentoring on parenting efficacy and empowerment, especially the empowerment of Black mothers raising children on their own. Indeed, the very definition of youth mentoring, having a caring and thoughtful person in the youth's life to help them thrive, may unintentionally send a message to parents that they need help in raising their children, which can lead to disempowerment. While the youth mentoring literature asserts that mentoring does not take over the role of parents, and mentors are only present to provide social and/or educational access to youth who without mentoring it would not have access, the entire aspect of youth mentoring, taken from a paternalistic, middle-class, white culture, sets up a deficit approach when considering the parenting practices of Black, female-led families.

To this end, the goal of this chapter is to explore the contradictions of the youth mentoring discourse regarding the parenting practices of Black mothers raising children on their own using data collected from a mentoring program designed to help youth with social and academic development. This mentoring program does great work for the youth with whom they work. The parents involved in the mentoring program having nothing but positive things to say about the program and the benefits of the program to their children. Indeed, both quantitative and qualitative data from the program show that the youth are more involved in school, have improved grades, and the program boasts a 100% graduation rate of all children involved in the program. However, I believe that the while the program is effective in its goal of mentoring youth, the

© KONINKLIJKE BRILL NV, LEIDEN, 2019 | DOI: 10.1163/9789004407985_007

discourse around parenting practices created from this mentoring program can paint a negative portrait of parents of color, specifically, Black mothers, that continues to uphold the stereotypes that exist around Black mothers and parenting practices. While data was gathered from interviews with mentors, parents, and youth involved in the program, I discuss how the language used around youth mentoring is actually disempowering to the parenting practices of the Black mothers involved in this study, using the discourse of the mentors. Purposively for this chapter, the discourse from two mentors from the program is examined.

Critical discourse analysis (CDA) will be used to explore the relationship between youth mentoring and parenting. A key concept of using CDA focuses on how language mediates relationships of power and privilege in social interactions (Rogers, Malancharuvil-Berkes, Mosley, Hui, & Joseph, 2005). Specifically, CDA allows for a deeper exploration of how the mentors tend to view the parenting practices of Black mothers. Further, using CDA demonstrates the cycle of privilege that exists related to how one views "good" parenting. However, in order to understand why CDA is needed to understand and explore how the discourse around mentoring perpetuates the cycle of power and privilege in youth mentoring and parenting, youth mentoring must first be defined, along with a discussion on Black families and parent involvement.

## 2     Mentoring Defined

Larose and Tarabulsy (2005) define mentoring as a "sustained relationship between an individual with experience (the mentor) and an individual with less experience (the protégé) in which the mentor provides the protégé with different types of support" (p. 440). Mentoring is used in a variety of different fields and different types of mentoring exist, but the one constant in youth mentoring is that parents are often left out of the mentoring equation. The youth mentoring literature mostly focuses on the mentor-youth dyads and the perspectives of parents are absent (Rhodes, 2002; Spencer, Basualdo-Delmonico, & Lewis, 2011). Indeed, Philip, Shucksmith, and King (2004) conducted a qualitative study and found that mentors preferred to interact with their mentee instead of involving the families. Although an overwhelming amount of research demonstrates the positive influences that families have when they are more involved with their children, it is puzzling that the role of parents have not been explored. It seems that one area of mentoring that continues to be overlooked is the involvement of the parents in the mentoring process. This can be extremely detrimental to Black families, especially as the discourse around parent involvement in Black families is deemed insufficient or nonexistent.

## 3    Parental Involvement and Black Families

Prins and Willson Toso (2008) state that the dominant discourse of parent involvement stipulates that good parents support their children's education in ways deemed appropriate by school staff; basically, falling in line with the school's definition of parent involvement. The issue that follows then, is what happens to parents who do not support their children's education in ways that the schools deem appropriate? These parents are often considered not invested in the educational outcomes of their children (Chavkin, 1993; Fields-Smith, 2009). On the contrary, Black parents are involved in their children's education in a variety of ways, such as engaging in frequent and meaningful conversations with their children, helping with homework, having clear and consistent behavioral rules for their children, providing support and motivation, expressing clear graduation expectations, and cultivating better parent-teacher relationships (Abdul-Adil & Farmer, 2006; Jackson & Remillard, 2005; Vondra, 1999). Just as important, research shows that black parents demonstrate parent involvement through racial socialization, or messages and practices that parents use to help shape their children's attitudes and understanding about the impact of race (Caughy, O'Campo, Randolph, & Nickerson, 2002; McKay, Atkins, Hawkins, Brown, & Lynn, 2003; Murray & Mandara, 2002). The disconnect, then, is that schools tend to view parent involvement in more school-based terms, as in volunteering, fund-raising, and attending parent-teacher conferences when requested (Lawson, 2003; Simoni & Adelman, 1993), while Black families tend to spend more time in home-based activities with their children and can view setting clear and consistent behavioral rules for their children as a form of parent involvement (Abdul-Adil & Farmer, 2006).

These opposing views are not surprising, as historically, Black families have been viewed through a deficit perspective, often viewed as disadvantaged and uneducated, especially if coming from a single-parent, female-led household (McAdoo & Younge, 2009). This constitutes a problem as one half of all Black families are female led (U.S. Census, 2003), and poverty is highest in female led, single parent households (McAdoo & Younge, 2009). Further exacerbating this problem is the fact that middle class European American's values and practices are often viewed as the standard for normative functioning (McAdoo & Younge, 2009). Yet, discourse on parent involvement continues to center on how to increase the parent involvement of Black, low-income, and other families of color. As parent involvement strategies are largely based on school cultures that are formed from middle-class, European-American cultural norms (Fields-Smith, 2007; Freeman, 2010; Hill & Craft, 2003; Lee & Bowen, 2006),

Black families continue to remain disadvantaged and thusly, disempowered, when it comes to parental involvement.

This trend of viewing Black families as disadvantaged also exists when it comes to mentoring Black children, in that mentors are provided to help students who are deemed to need the support and encouragement they do not receive at home. The very purpose of youth mentoring may unintentionally set up a system of disadvantage and disempowerment towards Black parenting. Indeed, Yosso (2005) states:

> If one is not born into a family whose knowledge is already deemed valuable, one could then access the knowledges of the middle and upper class and the potential for social mobility through formal schooling. Bourdieu's theoretical insight about how a hierarchical society reproduces itself has often been interpreted as a way to explain why the academic and social outcomes of People of Color are significantly lower than the outcomes of Whites. The assumption follows that People of Color 'lack' the social and cultural capital required for social mobility. As a result, schools most often work from this assumption in structuring ways to help 'disadvantaged' students whose race and class background has left them lacking necessary knowledge, social skills, abilities and cultural capital. (p. 70)

In the same vein, mentors can often work from an assumption that Black youth from female-led, households lack the knowledge, skills, and abilities to properly parent their children or help their children become academically successful. I demonstrate this through the examination of the discourse used by two White mentors of Black children from female-led households.

## 4 Method and Analysis

Over the past few months, I was part of a research team evaluating a mentoring program of a local school district. The program has high regard from the school district and current data also shows the benefits of the program. Students are paired in the 4th grade with a mentor from the district and remain with the mentor through graduation, if at all possible. Referrals for the program are made from the school social worker, school counselor, or school psychologist. Those who stay in the program through graduation and are accepted into college receive a small scholarship. Parents of the students who are mentored are required to do three things: (1) attend two parent-teacher conferences, (2) attend one after school event, and (3) attend two parent education programs provided by the mentoring program.

The qualitative portion of the data collection included interviewing current and former mentors, current and former students, and current and former parents of the mentoring program. Interviews occurred in various locations that were conducive to the participants. My role as part of the research team was to conduct interviews with the mentor, the mentee, and the parents, or what we call, the triad. I also observed mentor training sessions and parent education sessions. The interviews used for this study were conducted at the mentors' homes. The mentor interviews lasted one hour and were done separately from the mother and youth participants. Data was analyzed using CDA.

## 5 Critical Discourse Analysis (CDA)

Fairclough (2003) states that CDA can be used to examine how discourses can produce or reproduce unequal power relationships, which can then perpetuate the concerning problem. I use CDA to explore the discourse around Black mothers' parenting practices through the eyes of the mentors. Doing this method of analysis allows for the examination of contradictions, specifically, the tendency to position parents as both resources and problems within the discourse of mentoring. Discourses are often based on the norms of a group and can lead to an exclusion and devaluing of the norms and practices of other groups, which in turns, leads to dominant discourses having the most power (Lai & Vadeboncoeur, 2012). Using CDA is appropriate for this study because as previously mentioned, Black parents are often viewed through a deficit lens as far as parenting and parent involvement. To examine the contradictions in youth mentoring using this approach, I first examined the pocket guide for volunteers of the program, followed by a critical examination of interview data using the transcribed interviews of two mentors. I looked for specific examples of discourse related to parenting and families and how the discourse around these topics re (produce) dominance, or the expert-learner theme in parent involvement. I assert that while this view of parenting does not directly harm the relationships among parents, mentors, or mentees, it can unintentionally disempower Black mothers by negating their parenting practices.

## 6 The Mentoring Pocket Guide

The mentoring pocket guide outlines the goals and mission of the program and specifies the roles and responsibilities of the mentors, mentees, and their families. The mission of the program is to "establish supportive relationships between adults and children, to broaden children's visions of their future, consequently helping them reach their fullest academic, physical, emotional and social potential." The phrases "broadening children's visions of their future" and "helping them reach their fullest ... potential" can imply to mentors that their mentees may not have a clear picture of their future, or that it needs to be expanded. This, then, also can imply that mentees' parents may not be able to provide this. These phrases immediately set up an expert-learner type of relationship between the family and the mentor, and could lead mentors to believe that the parents are not qualified or prepared to help their own children achieve success.

The messages received from the manual can be seen as contradictory in that the discourse in the manual both validates and discounts the role of parents in the mentoring relationship. While the training manual stresses that mentors do not take on the role of the parent and that an effective mentoring relationship is one that includes the support of the mentee's family (validation), throughout the training manual, the roles of parents remain absent (discounts). For example, the training manual states that effective mentors get to know the students and use the program staff to build stronger mentoring relationships. The manual does not mention the role of parents in these endeavors. Further, the training manual states that one factor that places students at risk of academic failure is little to no parent involvement, setting up the perception that some parents may not be involved. Additionally, while the manual lists the characteristics of families that could most benefit from a mentoring relationship, (e.g., the family must support education, must be aware of their responsibilities with the program and open to working as a team with the mentor), the tips for a successful mentoring relationship do not include working or collaborating with parents.

In summary, while I strongly believe that this youth mentoring program does help youth in need, it also unintentionally supports a system of power by reinforcing the beliefs that youth in need come from families that cannot and do not provide the proper parenting that leads to social, emotional, or academic success, as conveyed by the following statement taken from the training manual, "Children who have demonstrated an unmet potential are selected for this program. The evidence of this potential may be an expressed interest, a demonstrated talent, a desire for enriching activities or the promise of better academic performance. They are children who need the energies of *another* adult to achieve the potential within themselves" (p. 28). Again, I stress that youth mentoring and this youth mentoring program in general, is effective in helping youth find success in and out of school, but the view of parents that it sends, albeit unintentionally, can lead to parent disempowerment. I demonstrate this by examining the discourse of two mentors of the program, who

PARENTING PRACTICES OF BLACK, FEMALE-LED FAMILIES        151

worked with mentees from Black, female-led families. The names have been changed to protect the identity of the participants.

## 7 An Examination of Parent Perceptions through the Eyes of Two Mentors

### 7.1 *Interview—Sharon (mentor), Michelle (mentee), Mary (mother)*

Sharon is a White, married woman, in her fifties, with two grown children and lots of grandkids. She decided to work as a mentor after seeing the relationship that existed between a family friend and his mentee. Sharon became a mentor to Michelle, a Black female from a female-led household, when Michelle was in the 4th grade. Sharon stayed a mentor to Michelle through Michelle's graduation. Michelle was Sharon's only mentee. Sharon viewed Mary, Michelle's mother, as not having the parenting practices that were necessary for raising children to value independence and academic success. I present the following excerpts from Sharon's experience as a mentor when discussing Mary. These excerpts continually uphold the dominant viewpoint around parent involvement-that those whose parenting practices do not align with White, middle class social values, are seen as uninvolved, or not invested in their child's education. For example:

> At one point, I was picking up Michelle every day from school and she was coming to our house for dinner and homework, and then I would drop her off. But she kept her family separate. She didn't want her mom to know anything that was going on when we had her. I think Michelle felt she was protecting her mother, protecting her privacy. I also think her mom didn't want to let her kids be in this program, but felt she had no choice. Her son was also a mentee. I think her mother felt that we, the mentors, were interfering with her child-rearing. But the mom never followed through with anything. For example, Michelle was getting into trouble by not doing her homework and this was affecting her grades, but her mom couldn't get her to do the work. I had no trouble getting Michelle to do her work at my home. When she was coming over to our home every day, her grades dramatically improved. Her mom was nice, never rude or unwelcoming; I just felt that she thought we were intruding.

Here, Sharon shares her perceptions of Michelle's mother. Already, the tone of the conversation sets us an expert-learner dynamic. While saying the mother was always nice and never rude, Sharon also explicitly states that Mary is unable to help her daughter educationally nor keep her daughter out of trouble. She also assumed that Mary felt she was interfering in her role as a parent. When I asked, "Did you ever invite her mother and her siblings to go with you on trips or invite them to your home?," Sharon replied, "She could never go on activities. She was always working all day and night to make ends meet." This discourse portrays a type of privilege in parenting-the privilege of having time to do activities with kids, which Mary does not have. While Sharon had the means and the time to take Michelle on trips and do things with her, Mary has to spend all her extra time working just to "make ends meet." Although Sharon was simply stating a fact of how Mary had to work and Sharon viewed Mary's work ethic as a strength, it was also used as a contradiction of good parenting in that Sharon saw it as a reason that Michelle needed a mentor-Mary was always working so a mentor was needed for Michelle to offer her opportunities and activities that she would not have received otherwise. What is troubling about this discourse is not that Michelle needed a mentor to offer her opportunities, but that Mary was overlooked in this process. Basically, what Mary needs, and what Mary fails to receive, is social capital or the sharing of norms and resources in order to advance individual or group goals (Coleman, 1988). Those that have social capital have the knowledge, norms, and in this case, the resources, to help their children, and this is something that Mary does not have, and even through mentoring, social capital is passed to her daughter and Mary is overlooked. This continues to put her in a system of disadvantage because although Mary works all day to make ends meet, it is not enough to provide Michelle with what she needs. However, with social capital, Mary could have more knowledge to help her daughter become successful. The current mentoring format means that Michelle will always have to rely on others to provide certain knowledge instead of turning to her own mother, essentially disempowering Mary as a mother. Furthermore, what Mary does provide and teach her daughter—hard work, perseverance, facing hardships—is not viewed by Sharon as a form of parent involvement or a sign of investment in Michelle's future. This excerpt supports Collin's (2009) assertion that working Black women do not align with traditional family ideals that include the role of the mother being at home with their children, "Everything the imagined traditional family ideal is thought to be, Black families are not" (p. 53).

In another excerpt, Sharon explains how she helps Michelle. Sharon mentions the things she teaches Michelle, which implies that Michelle did not learn these from her own family:

> I tried to teach Michelle things that could help her in life-to not be so judgmental, to broaden her views on the people she saw. I took her to

PARENTING PRACTICES OF BLACK, FEMALE-LED FAMILIES     153

nice dinners. Taught her how to shake hands and make eye contact. I taught her not to gossip so much, and we discussed movies and books. I taught her social skills. She taught me how to see the world from a different perspective and how to endure things that you are not having fun with and how to stick through things that you do not like; remember, this relationship was not what I expected but I stayed with Michelle. Also, through Michelle, I got the chance to meet people that I ordinarily wouldn't have-people outside of the university. I also learned from her how to keep going-they (Michelle and her siblings) overcame a lot of their mom's mistakes and they kept going. But her mom does work hard and love her children.

Also, Sharon admits that Mary loves her children, but she also mentions that the children had to overcome the mother's mistakes. This statement alone exemplifies a more negative view of Mary's parenting practices—while working hard to support the kids is fine, Mary also makes a lot of mistakes as a mother. Sharon's view of parenting is similar to the historical view of Black parenting, particularly female-led households, namely, that their parenting skills are not considered good enough. Further, Sharon mentions all that she taught Michelle, who was in the 4th grade when she began the program: social skills, not being judgmental, making eye contact. These all behaviors Sharon deems in appropriate in Michelle—behaviors that Michelle must have learned from her home, then, are wrong and need to be changed.

Sharon goes on to say about Mary:

You know, I had to give up my dreams on this relationship. I stayed with Michelle through the end and never gave up trying. I think her mom had a negative influence on her and her siblings. I think she didn't want her kids to succeed because she thought they would leave her. As it was, even though Michelle went to college, she dropped out after one year and moved back home with her mother. Michelle didn't want to be away from her mother.

Even here, the discourse on parenting is framed through a negative lens— Mary having a negative influence on her kids. Even if Sharon is correct about Mary not wanting her daughter to go away to college, who gets to decide if this is negative? Is it not okay to want to attend school near home to stay near one's family? Nevertheless, I believe that Sharon does not intentionally negate Mary's parenting practices, but as so often with the dominant discourse of privilege, behaviors and actions that fall outside of the view of normalcy, are simply seen as wrong. What Sharon seems to be doing at this point aligns with Lightfoot's (2004) assertion around parent involvement programs, that "these programs implicitly assume that the best possible outcome for participating parents and their children is for the pattern of family interactions to come to resemble that of White, middle- or upper-class, English-speaking families as closely as possible" (p. 100).

When asked about the impact of racial differences on the mentoring relationship, it is interesting that Sharon explicitly states feeling that the differences in race had an effect on the relationship and she was careful about "not insulting Michelle's mother or negating the role of her mother."

> I also tried to help out at the school by trying to get the teachers to see things from Michelle's point of view and help them not be so hard on her mother. I told them, 'the mom works hard, but she can't be a teacher and know how to develop programs.' I even covered for the mom for Michelle's benefit. I didn't like to see her mom talked about so negatively.

Through this discourse, Sharon is aware of racial differences and is aware of the negative views that the school holds regarding Mary. However, this discourse aligns with how society views Black mothers-not providing the proper care, guidance, and nurturance needed to help their children be successful (Rosenthal, 1999). Interestingly, while Sharon is aware that the school holds negative views of Mary, Sharon is unaware of the negative views that she herself hold—for example, "the mom can't be a teacher" or "know how to develop programs." This unawareness is often what continues to contribute to the continued negative view of Black parenting, particularly Black mothers' capability to be "proper" parents. Indeed, Lightfoot (2004) asserts, "the individuals being called have been selected on the basis of their perceived lack of skills to raise their children properly or to help them succeed academically, rather than on the basis of any positive qualities they may have" (p. 102). It can be disempowering to Black mothers, at a time when we need to actually empower mothers and their families. Instead, it as Collins (2009) state, "portraying African American women as stereotypical mammies, matriarchs, welfare recipients, and hot mommas helps justify U.S. Black women's oppression" (p. 76). On the contrary, Black families, and particularly mothers, have a number of strengths that they bring to parenting that tend to be overlooked.

Sharon was a very nice and an extremely friendly person and I truly believe she had nothing but good intentions for Michelle while she worked with her, but she viewed Mary through a deficit lens and found her lacking. I wonder what might have happened if Sharon tried just as hard to ingrain herself into

PARENTING PRACTICES OF BLACK, FEMALE-LED FAMILIES 155

Michelle's family and way of being, for example, having dinner at her house or going to church with Michelle and her family, especially as Michelle seemed to have a strong bond with her mother. What if she developed a relationship with Mary first and had open communications with her about issues related to race, to mothering, to education, to mentoring? What may have happened if instead of omitting Mary excluding her from the mentoring relationship, Sharon had developed a mentoring relationship that included both Mary and Michelle? What if Sharon has asked Mary to share her thoughts and feelings about college and her own goals she had for Michelle?

Family can be a strong influence in Black families as Sharon realized through mentoring Michelle. Sharon bemoaned the lack of relationship between her and Michelle, and blamed Mary for the weak relationship. As Michelle had a strong bond with her mother, Sharon may have approached the mentoring relationship the wrong way. I believe Sharon was able to provide new experiences and opportunities to which Michelle would not ordinarily have access. However, while Sharon had good intentions, for her, mentoring was about helping a child overcome negative experiences and providing experiences and knowledge that she felt was needed in order to be successful. The problem is that the overall discourse around mentoring that Sharon used led to the continued negative view point of the parenting practices of Black mothers, especially when it involved education. This negative view is also demonstrated in the following interview.

### 7.2 Interview—Donny (Mentor), Susan (Mother), Joey (Mentee)

Donny, a White male, currently mentors a 13-year-old Black male student, Joey. His discourse around Susan, Joey's mother, is also tinged with negativity. The theme that repeatedly arises from Donny's discourse on Susan was her lack of stressing academic success for Joey. For example, when discussing helping Joey with his grades, he says:

> I try to do what I can to get him focused on school. He also doesn't have, his mother doesn't have an Internet connection at home, so I've been talking to her about that. You know, she is a great mom and we have a great relationship and all of that, um, but I think it's important for kids at home these days to be able to do research, you know, science for example is one of his worst classes, that's where he's getting a C. Well, that's where the Internet would lend itself to—amazingly well in terms of allowing him to do research. So I don't know what the issue is. It's been many, many months since she just hasn't had an Internet connection and I keep asking her about it.

To Donny, having the Internet is important for academic success, and he does not understand why Susan will not obtain access to the Internet, for the sake of her son's academic success. When I raised the issue of money, Donny replied that Joey has a cell phone and the Internet is more valuable than paying a monthly cell phone bill. So here, the discourse implies that Susan's priorities are not where they should be, and also implies that Susan's parenting practices does not prioritize education.

Donny's view of Susan's lack of focus on education is also evident in the following statement, "I think Joey listens to his mother. Like I said, I do worry about the impact of his brother. I worry about, I don't think his mom takes Joey—and this is just a complete guess—but she doesn't take his academic success as seriously as I think she needs to. You know, she should have—forgo other things, and have an Internet connection." Here, the discourse again demonstrates the negative view of Susan's priorities as it relates to education. This view is again evident as he explains how he feels about Susan not making Joey attend summer school.

> The school recommended that he go to summer school. Now his grades were good, well, decent—you know, I wouldn't say good, but decent enough that she went and petitioned the school to get him out of summer school. And if it was up to me, I would've sent him to summer school. He's got clear weaknesses in math, I'll see them, like I do practices problems with him sometimes, and I can see things that he understands, doesn't understand, and the kid—you know, he needs to go to summer school. And it's been two years in a row it's been like that. He pushes back, like he'll say, "Oh, I wanna play basketball and I need a summer," but you know, the school is saying, "well you need to be in summer school." But what she can do, I guess, as every parent can go and petition the school and if he's had good, decent, grades, they can get out of it. But you know, I don't think it would hurt him to be in summer school versus hanging around. She's an only parent so most of the days he's gonna be on his own. He is at home alone.
>
> In fact, even today, through the whole Spring Break, that's why I'm going to call him today because he's at home alone. And what kind—he can get into all kinds of trouble or just, you know I call him and say, "What are you doing?" "Nothing." That's almost one hundred percent of the response all the time. And I would buy him books, I try to buy him books on things I think he'd been interested in, and he does read them. But for most of the time he's playing video games, or watching basketball and non-supervised. Um, so I think his mom could do a lot more to reinforce the importance of getting good grades and his academics and things like

## PARENTING PRACTICES OF BLACK, FEMALE-LED FAMILIES 157

> that. I find even um, the parent-teacher meetings I've been to, um, a lot of times, the teacher—I think the teachers are in some way afraid of her. You know, it's like they are afraid to say anything negative because it's like she's going to be defensive.

Interestingly, when asked what values Susan does teach Joey, Donny replies,

> I don't know for sure, I think, his mom makes sure that he dresses well, so he's always like, well kept, which is nice and well groomed. I think she—they all inadvertently they are teaching him that education is not that important. His older brother did fine without it, his mother doesn't reinforce certain things, so he's learning that, not because it's proactive but because inadvertently by things they are not doing to stress the importance of it.

Again, Donny voices his disapproval of Susan's parenting practices regarding education and when asked about the values that Susan does hold, Donny could only think of a non-academic value. She does not reinforce it or stress the importance of it, and according to Donny, education should be stressed and should be one of the most important things that Susan can teach Joey. It is interesting that Donny believes the family is negating the importance of education as this supports the literature regarding Black parent involvement which states the negative perception that Blacks are uninvolved in their children's education. As with Mary in the first example, Susan's lack of adherence to what the mentor considers important, implies that her parenting practices need to be improved, and leads to the reason their children need mentors.

## 8 Implications

Overall, the mentoring program is an excellent resource for youth and is demonstrated to be effective. However, I believe these two interviews exemplify the following negative viewpoints that can occur with youth mentoring and Black parenting:

1. I can provide better opportunities for your child.
2. I can teach your child what they need to be successful.
3. I can help your child learn better ways of being.
4. My way of being, doing, thinking, is better than your way.

These views are evident in the language used by the two mentors. What is especially disheartening is that the majority of youth who are deigned as needing mentors come from low-income families and families of color, while most mentors are White. The system of power that exists in these mentoring relationships often goes unnoticed. This unintentional disempowerment that occurs can be harmful to the families and children. However, specific research needs to be done on the impact of mentoring on parental efficacy and parent empowerment. Further, more research needs to be done on the impact of cross-cultural mentoring on parental efficacy and parent empowerment. Specifically in this chapter, both mentors are not only racially different than their mentors, but they also come from different social classes with the mentors being from middle to upper middle class families, while the mentees were from lower social economic statuses. However, specifically for mentoring programs, and specifically this program, I believe that certain things need to occur to circumvent the negative perceptions and discourse around parenting. To this end, I offer two major strategies that can be used to help mentors reconceptualize the role of Black parents and can also be used to help mentors begin to think differently about their views on Black parenting practices.

## 9    Reconceptualizing the Role of Black Mothers and Parenting Practices

This program, and others like it, needs to expand their training sessions to include modules on understanding culturally diverse families, which should include developing cultural awareness and building trust especially as the inclusion of a parental component should be an important aspect. Indeed, parental support and involvement is considered a best practice that leads to positive results in the youth mentoring process (Rhodes & Spencer, 2005).

*Develop cultural awareness.* This goes beyond mentors learning about the families with whom they will be working, but more so about becoming aware of their own assumptions, beliefs, and worldviews about Black families and their parenting skills. Mentoring programs should include a component that allows for mentors to explore their values, biases, preconceived notions, and stereotypes they hold in order to work more effectively with Black families (Kalyanpur & Harry, 1997). Further, it would be helpful to require mentors to meet on a monthly basis to reflect and discuss their reactions to certain things they have seen and heard in the process of working with their mentee. This meeting can help with pointing out when mentors privilege the values, voice, and norms of White middle-class families over their mentee's family (Cooper, 2009; Noguera, 2003).

PARENTING PRACTICES OF BLACK, FEMALE-LED FAMILIES          159

*Building trust.* Building trust calls for mentors to value and demonstrate respect for Black values, beliefs, and attitudes. A major method of building trust is to have open and honest communications with their mentee's family about everything, including value conflicts, assumptions, and goals and expectations. Open communication creates collaborative relationships and can take away the power differential in a mentoring relationship. For example, Donny could have been honest in sharing his feelings on the need for an Internet connection over a cell phone, allowing for Susan to share her reasons for using her money to pay for a cell phone instead of a monthly Internet connection. Sharon could have asked Mary about her goals and expectations for her daughter. If she did want Mary to stay close to home, Sharon could have been a great resource in working with Mary and Michelle together to research higher education options that were nearby.

## 10      Conclusion

I understand that my stance on mentoring and Black mothering may be unique. Indeed, I shared a draft of this chapter with three professors, two of whom were White females, and one White male and the feedback was overwhelmingly negative. They disagreed with my view of how mentoring disempowers Black mothers and felt that this viewpoint actually contributes to racism. While initially hurt and dismayed over the comments, it did enable me to step back and take a look at the larger picture. After all, maybe I could not see clearly because I am Black, raised by a single mother, in a low-income environment; maybe I am not being objective in my analysis of the data. However, one tenet of CDA is that discourse analysis is interpretive (Wodak, 1996), and this is the way that I, the researcher, interpret the data. I wholeheartedly agree that someone else may interpret it differently. Further, the goal of CDA is to disrupt discourses and challenge the passive acceptance of the status quo (Rogers et al., 2005). I believe my viewpoint does disrupt the discourse around mentoring and challenges the passive acceptance of the benefits of mentoring on at-risk youth. I hope that this chapter can be used to challenge the negative perceptions of parenting that continues to surround Black mothers to, as Collins (2009) assert, "form positive self-definitions in the face of derogated images of Black womanhood" (p. 102), or in this case, Black motherhood. Youth mentoring is an effective route to helping to break down barriers to academic success of at-risk youth, but it can also disempower parents in the process. I hope this chapter can be used to change the discourse around mentoring from negating the parenting practices of Black mothers to embracing all they have to offer.

## References

Abdul-Adil, J. K., & Farmer Jr., A. D. (2006). Inner-city African American parental involvement in elementary schools: Getting beyond urban legends of apathy. *School Psychology Quarterly, 21,* 1–12.

Caughy, M. O., O'Campo, P. J., Randolph, S., & Nickerson, K. (2002). The influence of racial socialization practices on the cognitive and behavioral competence of African American preschoolers. *Child Development, 73,* 1611–1625.

Chavkin, N. (Ed.). (1993). *Families and schools in a pluralistic society.* Albany, NY: State University of New York Press.

Coleman, J. S. (1988). Social capital in the creation of human capital. *The American Journal of Sociology, 94,* S95–S120.

Collins, P. H. (2009). *Black feminist thought.* New York, NY: Routledge.

Cooper, C. W. (2009). Parent involvement, African American mothers, and the politics of educational care. *Equity and Excellence in Education, 42,* 379–394.

DuBois, D. L., Holloway, B. E., Valentine, J. C., & Cooper, H. (2002). Effectiveness of mentoring programs for youth: A meta-analytic review. *American Journal of Community Psychology, 30,* 157–197.

DuBois, D. L., & Silverthorn, N. (2005). Characteristics of natural mentoring relationships and adolescent adjustment: Evidence from a national study. *Journal of Primary Prevention, 26,* 69–92.

Fairclough, N. (2003). *Analyzing discourse: Textual analysis for social research.* New York, NY: Longman.

Fields-Smith, C. (2009). After "it takes a village": Mapping the terrain of Black parental involvement in the post-Brown era. In L. Tillman (Ed.), *The Sage handbook of African American education* (pp. 153–168). Thousand Oaks, CA: Sage Publications.

Freeman, M. (2010). 'Knowledge is acting': Working-class parents' intentional acts of positioning within the discursive practice of involvement. *International Journal of Qualitative Studies in Education, 23,* 181–198.

Hill, N. E., & Craft, S. A. (2003). Parent-school involvement and school performance: Mediated pathways among socioeconomically comparable African American and Euro-American families. *Journal of Educational Psychology, 95,* 74–83.

Hudley, C. (2009). Academic motivation and achievement of African American youth. In H. A. Neville, B. M. Tynes, & S. O. Utsey (Eds.), *Handbook of African American psychology* (pp. 187–197). Thousand Oaks, CA: Sage Publications.

Jackson, K., & Remillard, J. (2005). Rethinking parent involvement: African American mothers construct their roles in the mathematics education of their children. *School Community Journal, 15,* 51–73.

Kalyanpur, M., & Harry, B. (1997). A posture of reciprocity: A practical approach to collaboration between professionals and parents of culturally diverse backgrounds. *Journal of Child and Family Studies, 6,* 487–509.

Lai, Y., & Vadeboncoeur, J. A. (2012). The discourse of parent involvement in special education: A critical analysis linking policy documents to the experiences of mothers. *Educational Policy, 27*, 867–897.

Larose, S., & Tarabulsy, G. M. (2005). *Academically at-risk students*. In D. DuBois & M. Karcher (Eds.), *The Sage program on applied developmental science: Handbook of youth mentoring* (pp. 440–454). Thousand Oaks, CA: Sage Publications.

Lawrence-Lightfoot, S. (1978). *Worlds apart: Relations between families and schools*. New York, NY: Basic Books.

Lawson, M. (2003). School-family relations in context: Parent and teacher perceptions of parent involvement. *Urban Education, 38*, 77–133.

Lee, J. S., & Bowen, N. (2006). Parent involvement, cultural capital, and the achievement gap among elementary school children. *American Educational Research Journal, 43*, 193–218.

Lightfoot, D. (2004). "Some parents just don't care": Decoding the meanings of parental involvement in urban schools. *Urban Education, 39*, 91–107.

LoSciuto, L., Rajala, A. K., Townsend, T. N., & Taylor, A. S. (1996). An outcome evaluation of across ages: An intergenerational mentoring approach to drug prevention. *Journal of Adolescent Research, 11*, 116–129.

McAdoo, H. P., & Younge, S. N. (2009). Black families. In H. A. Neville, B. M. Tynes, & S. O. Utsey (Eds.), *Handbook of African American psychology* (pp. 103–115). Thousand Oaks, CA: Sage Publications.

McGoldrick, M. (1982). Ethnicity and family therapy: An overview. In M. McGoldrick, J. K. Pearce, & J. Giordano (Eds.), *Ethnicity and family therapy* (pp. 3–30). New York, NY: Guilford.

McKay, M. M., Atkins, M. S., Hawkins, T., Brown, C., & Lynn, C. J. (2003). Inner-city African American parent involvement in children's schooling: Racial socialization and social support from the parent community. *American Journal of Community Psychology, 32*, 107–114.

Murray, C., & Mandara, J. (2002). Racial identity in African American children: Cognitive and experimental antecedents. In H. P. McAdoo (Ed.), *Black children: Social educational and parental environments* (pp. 73–96). Thousand Oaks, CA: Sage Publications.

Noguera, P. A. (2008). *The trouble with black boys and other reflections on race, equity, and the future of public education*. San Francisco, CA: Jossey-Bass.

Philip, K., Shucksmith, J., & King, C. (2004). *Sharing a laugh? A qualitative study of mentoring interventions with young people*. London: Joseph Rowntree Foundation.

Prins, E., & Willson Toso, B. (2008). Defining and measuring parenting for educational success: A critical discourse analysis of the parent education profile. *American Educational Research Journal, 45*, 555–596.

Rosenthal, M. K. (1999). Out-of-home child care research: A cultural perspective. *International Journal of Behavioral Development, 23*, 477–518. doi:10.1080/016502599383928

Rhodes, J. E. (2002). *Stand by me: The risks and rewards of mentoring today's youth.* Cambridge, MA: Harvard University Press.

Rhodes, J. E. (2005). A model of youth mentoring. In D. L. Dubois & M. J. Karcher (Eds.), *Handbook of youth mentoring* (pp. 30–43). Thousand Oaks, CA: Sage Publications.

Rhodes, J. E., & Spencer, R. (2005). Someone to watch over me. Mentoring programs in the after-school lives of youth. In J. L. Mahoney, R. W. Larson, & J. S. Eccles (Eds.), *Organized activities as contexts of development: Extracurricular activities, after-school and community programs* (pp. 419–435). Mahwah, NJ: Erlbaum.

Rogers, R., Malancharuvil-Berkes, E., Mosley, M., Hui, D., & Joseph, G. O. (2005). Critical discourse analysis in education: A review of the literature. *Review of Educational Research, 75*, 365–416.

Rosenthal, M. K. (1999). Out-of-home child care research: A cultural perspective. *International Journal of Behavioral Development, 23*, 477–518.

Simoni, J. M., & Adelman, H. S. (1993). School-based mutual support groups for low-income parents. *Urban Review, 25*, 335–350.

Spencer, R., Basualdo-Delmonico, A., & Lewis, T. O. (2011). Working to make it work: The role of parents in the youth mentoring process. *Journal of Community Psychology, 39*, 51–59.

Tierney, J. P., Grossman, J. B., & Resch, N. L. (1995). *Making a difference. An impact study of big brothers/big sisters.* Philadelphia, PA: Public/Private Ventures.

Vondra, J. I. (1999). Commentary for "schooling and high-risk populations: The Chicago longitudinal study." *Journal of School Psychology, 37*, 471–479.

Wodak, R. (1996). *Disorders of discourse.* London: Longman.

Yosso, T. J. (2005). Whose culture has capital? A critical race theory discussion of community cultural wealth. *Race, Ethnicity and Education, 8*, 69–91.

CHAPTER 7

# Final Thoughts

*Juan F. Carrillo*

*First, a reflection:*

I used to help out with a high school soccer team. I was social studies teacher and have long been involved in sports. I recall students asking me to be the head soccer coach. Over time—I became in essence, an assistant coach. A bizarre reality considering that I did not grow up playing soccer. I was not coached on the game. I did love the game and it was my students that inspired me to play. I fell in love with the feeling, in the game, on the pitch, early in the cold morning, late in darkening night, in gain and in loss, in community there was some kind of community. It was hard for me to join adult leagues though as maneuvering around cookie cutter homes and hegemonic forms of whiteness of how the game was played in some of these places took away from the soul that I remembered while playing with and coaching high school youth. I cherished the conversations about life that gave me life, it gave me meaning about what soccer really is: a family, a coming together, and honest back and forth of how we can grow together and correct, grow, change and love more deeply. It was also a subaltern exercise in agency and freedom, the poetry of the soccer moves, the joking, the charisma, the skill, the beauty of movement, the speed, the hope of scoring a goal or making the perfect pass, these were some lessons in love. The score mattered, sure, but it was not the big picture in my little world. Year after year we were one of the top high school soccer teams in the state of Arizona. We were "high achievers" without completely selling out our souls. We won without letting go of roots, we won without letting go of that vibe-the radical place of freedom where adolescents from the barrio could be themselves without being fully demolished by the gaze of otherness. It was not always easy, but it was an act of defiance, a constant playfulness that did not leave rigor behind, but did make present the belief that we did not need to be fixed. Year after year, I remember being called, "Carrillo." Even in this writing there is controversy, I hope that I do not romanticize (and yet, why is the romantic bad?), I hope that I get to be something on the page that captures my moment, not just the process passed down in power-centric spheres of publishing.

What was so beautiful about that past, about coaching, was that *dialogue, reflexivity*, and *student-centered* realities came into the game. I got to know the

© KONINKLIJKE BRILL NV, LEIDEN, 2019 | DOI: 10.1163/9789004407985_008

164                                                                                      CARRILLO

students, the community, the families, the flow of youth in context, I was not
the college educated teacher trying to mold them into a bubble of assimilation.
I never fell short on being demanding in some ways, but it was with appreciation of how they showed up in spite of huge obstacles. I was inspired by their
dreams in spite of a toxic sociopolitical context in which they lived. I asked
them simple and important questions like: what do you want?

I tell this backdrop narrative to share how mentoring in general, the Gold Medal
Program, and related research can benefit from: dialogue, reflexivity, and student-centered approaches. I believe that all of this must take place within a serious
analysis of power as well. The chapters in this book remind us of the importance of
these elements. Below, I offer some additional discussion on these elements.

## 1    DRS (Dialogue, Reflexivity, Student-Centered) Mentoring

### 1.1    *Dialogue*

Dialogue must be part of the of mentoring program in critical ways. There
should be conversations that not only engage how to acquire middle class cultural capital but also dialogue pertaining to the stories of young people and
the assets that they bring to the table. Some of the chapters in this book point
out how mentoring without critical dialogue can be very problematic. Mentees
and all stakeholders need to have power, class, and all other forms of intersectionality in the open dialogue process so that a truly sustaining, holistic, and
empowering programs are created.

### 1.2    *Reflexivity*

It never ends. Students from marginalized communities will have to face how
those from the dominant group may seek to "civilize" them. Many have good
intentions. However, there must be a critical reflexivity process for mentors.
In many mentoring programs this process entails very little personal digging
into the story of the mentor even as there are power and historical imbalances.
Programs need to have training that addresses this issue. This may be uncomfortable, this may hurt, this may produce questions and ambiguities that dis-
orient initial ideas around mentoring. This process is crucial for working in
true community and within vulnerable, honest, and transparent links between
all those that are involved.

### 1.3    *Student-Centered*

Students need to be have an influential part in sharing what they want. While
the mission of some mentoring programs is about adding something "new" to

FINAL THOUGHTS 165

the mentee's life, these resources and opportunities can still be integrated with student voice and input. If not, toxic and dangerous forms of colonization can happen. These injuries can take shape even as "success" metrics may be met in some ways. There is always a bigger story beyond the numbers. There may be a production of a hidden pain even as the numbers look good.

## 2 Mentoring in Alternate Reality Systems (MARS)

I write this section at over 7,000 feet above sea level in Flagstaff, Arizona. It's in the 30's at night and in the 50's during the day. I got to see a shooting star. Ducks or maybe it was geese, ascend and descend over a nearby lake. Alicia Keys sings and sings as the car crosses over the town's hills. My oldest son "studies" Mars at the local university. He is a physics major. Mars, the red planet, the fascinating place of mystery and awe. Mars has a thin ozone layer. Folk talk about colonizing Mars. Mentoring in alternate realities is grounded in labeling the labels. It is grounded in quiet moments of desperation. It is grounded migration. It is grounded in suspicion. It is at times, existential. There is travel and different layers of gravity. The red is an ether of care, the hope of opportunity, the systemic critique, the wondering and avant-garde soul, the curious whisperer: there is a full person that you may not be seeing.

Mentoring in alternate reality systems (MARS) is space travel. This process recognizes that different lives are possible and valid. This process recognizes that we *ain't it*. This process has an honesty about the red planet, you look up, you see it next to the moon, you check yourself and are in awe of the bigger multiverse of creative genius that lies in that which we often overlook or see as not being important. I write this section as someone who was raised in working-class communities and had to please. I had to "succeed" within dominant society's frameworks to be human. Or so I was told. At middle age, I listen to a song by Maxwell and watch my soul take different takes on what happened.

MARS is far away. For many mentors, the time, access, and critical reflexivity is a distant thing. This chapter is writing itself or maybe I am the writer or maybe I am here or not really here. The person that mentors gets mentored too. Pay attention. Alternate realities teach. Borders of being and becoming. No program in the world should be a savior. I walk through communities in this mountain community of Flagstaff, Arizona as the White "pioneers" have murals all over town and people of color are forgotten. I talk to small business owners of color to learn about their imprints, many have roots going back over a century. In alternate realities there are multiple stories. Mentoring should not be about cleaning up a nuisance.

MARS is additive but it is also careful, hierarchies are balanced out. Stories have a place. The walk, the long walk, is beautiful and terrifying, the source, when not discussed, roots, when not discussed are immersed in new stories of erasure without a true place to be metaphor and wise. MARS is messy *because that is true.*